How to
Pray Like
JESUS
and the
Saints

How to
Pray Like

JESUS
and the
Saints

A STUDY GUIDE FOR CATHOLICS

By Fr. Alfred McBride, O.Praem.

Our Sunday Visitor Publishing Division
Our Sunday Visitor, Inc.
Huntington, Indiana 46750

Nihil Obstat: Rev. Michael Heintz, Ph.D.
Censor Librorum
Imprimatur: ✠ John M. D'Arcy
Bishop of Fort Wayne - South Bend
July 23, 2009

The *Nihil Obstat* and *Imprimatur* are official declarations that a book or pamphlet is free of doctrinal or moral error. No implication is contained therein that those who have granted the *Nihil Obstat* or *Imprimatur* agree with the contents, opinions, or statements expressed.

The Scripture citations used in this work are taken from the *Second Catholic Edition of the Revised Standard Version of the Bible* (RSV), copyright © 1965, 1966, and 2006 by the Division of Christian Education of the National Council of the Churches of Christ in the United States of America. Used by permission. All rights reserved.

English translation of the *Catechism of the Catholic Church* for the United States of America, copyright © 1994, United States Catholic Conference, Inc. — Libreria Editrice Vaticana. English translation of the *Catechism of the Catholic Church: Modifications from the Editio Typica,* copyright © 1997, United States Catholic Conference, Inc. — Libreria Editrice Vaticana.

The English translation of the Responsories and Non-Biblical Readings from the *Liturgy of the Hours* © 1974, International Committee on English in the Liturgy, Inc. All rights reserved.

Every reasonable effort has been made to determine copyright holders of excerpted materials and to secure permissions as needed. If any copyrighted materials have been inadvertently used in this work without proper credit being given in one form or another, please notify Our Sunday Visitor in writing so that future printings of this work may be corrected accordingly.

Our Sunday Visitor Publishing Division
Our Sunday Visitor, Inc.
200 Noll Plaza
Huntington, IN 46750
1-800-348-2440
bookpermissions@osv.com

ISBN: 978-1-59276-535-5 (Inventory No. T811)
LCCN: 2009929866

Cover design by Amanda Miller
Cover image: Jesus praying, detail from *The Prayer in the Garden of Gethsemane,*
Byzantine fresco (14th c.), Monastery Church, Ohrid, Macedonia
Photo: Erich Lessing / Art Resource, NY
Interior art: Hunt's *Light of the World,* The Granger Collection;
all other interior art, The Crosiers.
Interior design by Sherri L. Hoffman

PRINTED IN THE UNITED STATES OF AMERICA

Contents

The Holy Family (detail)

PREFACE

Our prayer journey begins with Jesus and ends with Mary. His mother taught him prayers in his childhood; Joseph took him to synagogue and modeled for him a life of devotion. The parents took him on pilgrimage to the Temple, where he participated in worship and the splendor of the ceremonies.

In his humanity, Jesus shows us how to pray before all important decisions. He also reminds us of the value of communal prayer, such as he practiced in the weekly synagogue services and at Temple liturgies. Beyond this, he invites us to join him in the deep, mysterious, silent prayer he offered to his Father in long periods in the desert and on the mountain. His prayer life was so remarkable that the apostles asked him to teach them how to pray like he did. Jesus responded by giving them the seven petitions of the *Our Father*, the most perfect oral prayer ever composed.

Central to his prayer were the Psalms — God's prayer book. The music and poetry of these revealed prayers resonated in his humanity with the divine world from which he came. So from earth, God the Father heard the Psalms from a humanity profoundly attuned to their origin and purpose. When we pray the Psalms at every Mass, we have the opportunity to sing them with Jesus and receive his blessings and proper attitude in doing so.

Our prayer journey next takes us to some high points in the story of prayer, from St. Augustine to modern times. The Lady Proba was one of the wealthiest women in the Roman Empire, a widow who migrated to a huge estate in Roman North Africa. A convert to Christianity, she sought spiritual guidance from

Augustine. His advice to the Lady Proba about prayer is relevant and practical, addressing issues such as the use of many words in praying, as well as wondering how God answers prayers.

In our coverage of St. Anselm's Soul Prayer, we focus on the role of faith in prayer. He teaches us, "We believe, that we may understand." We believe, that we may know the truth which sets us really free, a freedom that inclines us always to choose what is good for our lives and those around us. The soul of prayer is the faith that we are relating to God, the source of all we need to be fulfilled. When reading the Gospels, you need to allow your soul to long for God; to tell Our Lord that you thirst for his palpable presence, and that even your body yearns for him like a dry, weary land without water.

Next, we come to the dramatic story of St. Catherine of Siena, whose mystical communion with God was written down in her famous *Dialogues*. This is an aspect of prayer that can appeal to us. She was a woman who talked with God. We will often speak with God in our prayers, according to the gifts we receive. Catherine's prayer life taught her to love the Church and boldly rescue the Pope from the perils of Avignon. She also fed the poor, nursed the sick, and visited the prisoners. She was both a mystic and woman of practical charity. Powerful prayer makes powerful Christians who love God, the Church, and people in need.

Our next stop is with a soldier who learned how to pray after a wounded leg and three operations kept him in solitude until his new vocation became evident. St. Ignatius of Loyola spent several years growing up in deep prayer, which he translated into a practical guide known as *The Spiritual Exercises*. They have been one of the most influential guides to prayer for the last 400 years. We have chosen to highlight Jesuit Fr. Mark Link's adaptation of the Ignatian method for the everyday Catholic.

One of the most engaging mystics of all times is St. Teresa of Ávila. We call her an earthy mystic, since she had a way of never forgetting the basics of even the highest forms of prayer. In her view, we must never forget to return again and again to the figure of Christ in the Scriptures. Her point is that we can easily get caught in fantasy and delusion when we depart too far from the Incarnation. The highest rung on the ladder of prayer is always tied to the first step — an engagement with the incarnate Christ and the sacraments of the Church.

Today, it is popular to involve all the laity in the life of the Church and the call to holiness. It seems so new to us — yet in the seventeenth century, that is exactly what St. Francis de Sales accomplished. His secret was the capacity to adapt prayer to the many different types of people in the Church: the rich and poor, monks and soldiers, bishops and businessmen, mothers and mother superiors, busy people and the leisure class. Francis was a genius of discernment. He also was blessed with the gift of being a gentleman and a shrewd way of explaining the role of love in prayer.

Few saints in recent history have had the incredible appeal of St. Thérèse of Lisieux. Dead at twenty-four, barely more than nine years as a Carmelite, she gained an incomparable insight into the merciful love of God and a unique understanding of heaven. She fashioned an approach to prayer that told us it was a matter of small deeds and big love. She prophesied she would spend her time in heaven doing good on earth, confirming for us that the invisible wall that separates earth and heaven is pierced by prayer and explaining the communion of saints in a vivid and satisfying manner. We are not far away from each other. We are as close as a whispered prayer and saintly intercession.

In finding a way to pray with Mary, I chose her *Magnificat*. In those nine verses, we identify Mary with prayer at its supreme expression: joyful praise of God. Our Father loves us so much that he sent his Son to us to show us how to live, give us the power to achieve that life, and die to obtain the graces this requires. Most of Mary's recorded words are prayers. Her *Magnificat* is so eloquent that the Church sings it every night at Evening Prayer. Put on our lips, this prayer will recall how today Mary is called "blessed" more joyfully than at any time in history. She tells us the solution to pride is humility; the response to profanity is "Holy is his Name." Energized by prayer, our social conscience will call us to defend the poor, the hungry, and the unjustly treated. Prayer is both devotional and charitable and concerned about the defenseless.

Prayer, like love, is filled with many splendors which we report in these eleven brief chapters. I hope you find this more a tapestry than a monument. I have woven the strands of Catholic devotion together in such a way that our prayer heritage is available to widely different experiences of people in varying stages of growth. Most moments are small. All moments can be magnified by big love. If I have achieved this, then, I trust God will bless you and this work.

I am grateful to my book editor, Jackie Lindsey, and Our Sunday Visitor publisher, Greg Erlandson, for their encouragement and support in this project. May Jesus and Mary continue to walk with them.

Praise the Lord!

— Fr. Alfred McBride, O.Praem.
Easter 2008

One

JESUS PRAYS

In these days he went out to the hills to pray; and all night he continued in prayer to God.

— LK 6:12

And in the morning, a great while before day, he rose and went out to a lonely place, and there he prayed.

— MK 1:35

Jesus had a prayer life. The Gospels frequently report his devotion to prayer. When he prayed in the Jordan waters after his baptism, he heard his Father call him "beloved Son" and confirm his saving mission. He brought Peter, James, and John to the peak of Mount Tabor to pray. While he was absorbed in prayer, his face shone like the sun, and his clothes became white as snow. Once again, the voice of the Father acknowledged that Jesus is his beloved Son, to whom we should listen. When Jesus prays, his identity as Son of the Father leaps off the Scriptural page.

He sought solitude for prayer, often going to a deserted place or to the desert itself. In those sandy areas of deep silence, Jesus offered to his Father the needs and hopes of all people with whom he identified by becoming human. Before he began his public ministry, Jesus made a forty-day retreat in the desert. Fortified by prayer, he endured and repelled temptations by the devil. He wanted to become like us in all things except sin. His willingness to be tempted earned for us the power to overcome temptation:

For because he himself has suffered and been tempted, he is able to help those who are tempted.

— HEB 2:18

Prior to his choice of the apostles, Jesus prayed all night on a mountain — a place that speaks of communion with God. His call of the apostles was a prayer event. Pope Benedict says they were "begotten in prayer." And he kept praying for them, especially Peter. At the Last Supper, Jesus foretold Peter's denial, but also told him that he would pray for his repentance:

> *"Simon, Simon, behold, Satan demanded to have you, that he might sift you like wheat, but I have prayed for you that your faith may not fail; and when you have turned again, strengthen your brethren."*
>
> — Lk 22:31-32

How Did Jesus Learn to Pray?

The Son of God, becoming the Son of the Virgin Mary, learned to pray in his humanity. His last word on the Cross, "Father, into thy hands I commit my spirit" (Lk 23:46), was a customary prayer before going to sleep, taught him by his mother. She passed on to him many of the favorite prayers of her people. Mary also shared with him the wonders of God, on which she had meditated in her heart. Though we have no formal record of what Joseph may have taught Jesus, we can reasonably conclude that he would have taught his foster Son, by word and example, the reverence, attitudes, and rituals that accompanied holy meals at home and behavior at the synagogue.

Jesus learned the Psalms and canticles sung in the synagogue of Nazareth and the Temple in Jerusalem. The faith environment of his small hometown would shape his human heart with prayer for all occasions. The synagogue homilies prayerfully interpreted the Scriptural accounts of creation; the fall of Adam and Eve; the stories of the patriarchs, prophets, and kings; the great events of the Exodus; and the expectation of the Messiah. When the prophets were read at synagogue, Jesus heard the repeated Messianic yearnings of his people.

Jesus would learn prayer from the solemnity of weekly Sabbath meals and from the majesty of yearly Passover suppers, dwelling on the symbolism of the foods that recalled the Exodus from Egypt. At the age of twelve, he joined Mary and Joseph in a pilgrimage to Jerusalem. When he marched in the Temple processions, saw the sacrifices of paschal lambs, and lent his voice to the joyful music of the crowds praising God, his heart was touched and opened to what his Father desired. What liturgy and worship accomplished for the people found an exceptional resonance in the soul of the youthful Jesus.

On another pilgrimage to Jerusalem for the eight-day feast of Tabernacles (tents), the young Jesus, like other youth, would delight in camping out for eight days in tents made of branches and leaves. The feast celebrated the autumn harvest and called for ardent prayers for winter rains in preparation for the next planting. A water ceremony symbolized this need.

Jesus stood with the crowds gathered at the foot of Temple Mount, where a priest filled a golden bowl with water from the spring of Gihon. As one of the pilgrims, Jesus carried a myrtle branch in his right hand and a lemon in his left, to symbolize the harvest. With them, he followed the priest up the hill and sang, "With joy you will draw water from the wells of salvation" (Is 12:3). As an adult, Jesus returned to this feast and gave it its true meaning:

> "If any one thirst, let him come to me and drink. He who believes in me, as the Scripture has said, 'Out of his heart shall flow rivers of living water.'"
>
> — JN 7:37-38

The youthful Jesus marveled at the ritual of fire each evening. The night sky was ablaze with the festal torches in the

Court of Women on Temple Mount. Four golden candlesticks, so tall that ladders were needed to reach the tops, were capped with golden bowls of oil with lighted wicks floating in them. Choirs sang psalms of praise for God as a pillar of fire who encouraged their ancestors in the desert and was still their present light. In his adult ministry, Jesus returned to the feast and applied the fire ritual to himself:

> "I am the light of the world; he who follows me will not walk in darkness, but will have the light of life."
>
> — JN 8:12

Yet beyond this excellent formation, Jesus benefited from a secret source of prayer — his filial conversations with his Father. As he said to his worried parents when they found him in the Temple, "Did you not know I must be in my Father's house (Lk 2:49)?" The Father had always wanted a filial response from his sons and daughters. Now, in Jesus, his beloved Son, this would occur in his humanity with and for us. Finally on earth, a magnificent prayer rose from the purest and most innocent heart that ever existed in this world. At last, in the midst of humanity and from Jesus, the unimpeded conversation between Father and Son, so longed for by all the prophets, became a reality on earth.

How Did Jesus Teach Us to Pray?

Jesus showed us how to pray by his example. By praying formally in the synagogue and at the Temple, he witnessed the importance of liturgical prayer in union with the community of believers. In this kind of prayer, we are taught by the traditions of our people, not just today but from centuries past. The Church at worship is the haven and mother of prayer. In communion with the faith of God's people, we see the devotion of the worshipers and the richly moving rituals of Word and Sacrament in the celebration of the Eucharist. Above all, we learn in such prayer the movement of adoration to the Father, through the Son, in the Holy Spirit.

At the same time, Jesus witnessed the need for the prayer of solitude. He often retired to a mountain or a deserted place where, in silence, he could be in quiet communion with his Father. He sometimes spent an entire night in such meditative prayer. In one reported case he brought the apostles with him, so they could experience these hours of silent prayer, of yearning for union with God. They were so moved that afterwards they asked him to teach them to pray. Jesus responded to this request with the words of the greatest Christian prayer — the *Our Father.*

In his Sermon on the Mount, Jesus taught us that the first step in prayer is conversion of heart. This involves reconciliation with others whom we have injured, love for enemies, and a willingness to pray for those who persecute us. We should set time aside to pray to our Father in solitude and avoid empty words. We need to come before God with purity of heart, an attitude of forgiveness of others, and the resolve to humbly depend on God (Mt 5:21-26; 43-48; 6:5-15; 25-34).

Jesus tells us that once our hearts are converted to God, we learn to pray with faith. In Christ, we have the confidence to approach our Father as his beloved sons and daughters. Nothing seems impossible. With boldness, faith, and trust, we ask that we will be heard, so long as what we ask for is God's will (Mt 7:7-10). Jesus regretted his experience of "little faith" among those who had been blessed by being born in the community who passed onto them the faith of Abraham, Moses, and the martyred prophets — but he admired the faith of outsiders like the Roman centurion and the Canaanite woman. Today, Jesus is saddened by the "little faith" among his present followers and urges us to let the Holy Spirit set our faith on fire.

Hunt: The Light of the World

Finally, Jesus reminds us that we need to pray with persistence, patience, and humility. He tells the story of a man who goes to his friend at midnight, bangs on the door, and asks urgently for three loaves of bread to feed guests who have suddenly arrived. The friend protests that it is too late and the door is locked. But eventually, if he does not get up out of friendship

OPEN THE DOOR OF YOUR HEART

One of the most beloved artists of the Victorian era was Holman Hunt. In 1853, he completed his painting of Jesus as the "Light of the World." The painting shows Jesus, crowned with thorns and carrying a lantern, knocking at a door. The door is covered with vines and is weathered with age and disuse. Significantly, the door has no handle on the outside. It can be opened only from the inside.

The artist illustrated the words of Jesus:

"Behold, I stand at the door and knock; if any one hears my voice and opens the door, I will come in to him and eat with him, and he with me."

— Rev 3:20

This is Christ's call to prayer and an enduring relationship with him. Jesus does not force himself upon us. He knocks, but only we can open the door of our hearts — not just our minds. He knows there is a hunger for God in our hearts, and Jesus dramatizes the other truth — that he is continually in search of a relationship with us. In wanting to dine with us, Jesus offers the Eucharist as the most intimate way to achieve this goal.

The original painting hangs in Keble College, Oxford. So great was the demand to see it that Hunt painted a second much larger version in 1904. That copy toured the United Kingdom and many parts of the British Empire of those days, as well as the United States. Today, it hangs in St. Paul's Cathedral, London.

to give the bread, he will do so because of the persistence of his neighbor (Lk 11:5-13). If a human father knows how to give good gifts to his children, will not God be even more ready to hear our prayers, if they are for our good?

Jesus illustrated praying with patience with the parable of a widow who went to a dishonest judge, who feared neither God nor man, and demanded he render a just decision for her against her adversary. The judge delayed a long time, hoping she would go away, but she didn't — he feared she might even attack him! In the end, he gave her what she wanted so she would stop bothering him. Will not God, a just judge, be even more willing to hear our patient prayers (Lk 18:1-8)?

Jesus urges us to pray with humility. He illustrates this with the parable of the proud Pharisee and the humble tax collector. The Pharisee boasts that he is not greedy, dishonest, or adulterous, but fasts regularly and gives a tenth of his income to the Temple. The tax collector, with lowered eyes and a quiet whisper, humbly asks God to be merciful to him, a sinner. God was touched by the humility of the tax collector and answered his prayer (Lk 18:9-14).

Jesus knocks on the doors of our hearts and calls us to prayer. He wants a conversion of our hearts, a change in our selfish behavior, a revival of our faith and trust in him, a commitment to love God and neighbor. A conversion to a Christian lifestyle is the prelude, the power, and the result of prayer. Jesus teaches us to be persistent, patient, and humble in our praying. In giving us the seven petitions of the *Our Father*, Jesus provided us with the best outline of how to pray. This is the topic of our next chapter.

FOR REFLECTION

1. Why does Christ want a conversion of heart as a condition for prayer?
2. What is the role of faith and trust in the life of prayer?
3. Why do you need persistence, patience, and humility to pray effectively?
4. In meditating on the prayer experiences of Christ, which one speaks to you most?
5. When do you find yourself most in need of prayer?
6. Why must prayer be a habit and not just an occasional effort?

FOR CONTEMPLATION

He who knows what good things to give his children
exhorts us to ask, to seek and to knock.
The more we truly believe,
the more strongly we hope
and the more ardently we desire,
the more generously we will receive.
In our petitions we will receive more by sighs than by speech,
more by tears than by words.

— *LITURGY OF THE HOURS (LH)*
VOL. III, PP. 432-433

Two

THUS SHALL YOU PRAY:
THE *OUR FATHER*

He was praying in a certain place, and when he ceased, one of his disciples said to him, "Lord, teach us to pray."

— LK 11:1

Prayer "is the work of the heart, not of the lips, because God does not look at the words, but at the heart of him who prays."

— ABBOT SMARAGDUS (NINTH CENTURY),
DIADEM OF THE MONKS, 1

The seven petitions of the *Our Father* are crisp and short. Each petition invites interpretation and an application to our spiritual and moral lives. Throughout history, a number of famous saints have written commentaries on the *Our Father*. One of them was the martyr bishop, St. Cyprian of Carthage.

In his book on this prayer, Cyprian teaches us that in the *Our Father*, Christians are offered the right way of praying; he emphasizes that this prayer is said in the plural "so that whoever prays it, prays not for himself alone." In this chapter, we reflect on the *Our Father*, in the spirit of Cyprian and other saints throughout history.

Our Father, Who Art in Heaven

Christ directs us to say *Our Father*, not *My Father*. Jesus wants to be associated with each of us whenever we say this prayer. He also desires that we unite ourselves with the community of believers in the Body of Christ. Hence, this is both a personal and communal prayer. Jesus has a special reason for being with us whenever we say his prayer because it will find favor with the ear of the Father, who cannot fail to smile when he hears his Son's words. Because Christ has made us adopted sons and daughters of God, we can confidently bring our needs to our Father.

There is a story told about a wealthy man who had everything in life except children. In her late thirties, his wife bore him a son. She died soon after that. The little boy was physically weak, but his father loved him dearly, and even the woman who cooked his meals took a special interest in raising the child. Unfortunately, the boy died at the age of twelve; fortunately, his father had commissioned an artist to paint his picture. When the father died, before the will was read, the lawyer held up the small painting of the son and asked people to bid on it. He was met with silence; apparently, no one was interested. Then, at last, the poor cook raised her hand and bid ten dollars, and the lawyers gave her the picture and asked her to read the note on the back.

"Whoever seeks to own my beloved son," she read, "will receive all my treasure."

Hallowed Be Thy Name

God is infinitely holy, so we cannot pray that he become what he already is; in this petition, we actually ask that the holiness and the name of the Father become a reality in *our* lives. Scripture tells us that God wants us to be holy, free from sin, and filled with his love. "You shall therefore be holy, for I am holy" (Lev 11:45). St. Peter repeated this command of our Father for the Christian Church.

> But as he who called you is holy, be holy yourselves in all your conduct; since it is written, "You shall be holy, for I am holy."
> — 1 PET 1:15-16

The best way to be holy is to love God with all your heart and your neighbor as yourself. If you do this, you will avoid sin and honor God's name.

At World Youth Day 2004 in Cologne, one million young people gathered on the *Marienfeld* (Mary's Field) for Evening Prayer on Saturday night. Pope Benedict blessed a new bell honoring John Paul II. After the blessing, the bell was rung to call everyone to prayer and the resolve to be holy. The throng, representing nearly every country on earth, sang, "*Laudate Dominum, omnes gentes* — Praise the Lord, all you nations!" This was followed by a Holy Hour of adoration of the Blessed Sacrament. Then, the youth prepared for an all-night vigil to get ready for the morning celebration of the Eucharist. God was making his name holy in their hearts.

Thy Kingdom Come

Jesus preached frequently about the "kingdom of heaven" in his ministry. He did not say "kingdom of God" because Jews held that the name of God was too holy to be uttered, so "heaven" was a substitute. Jesus meant that he was establishing God's kingdom among us. It would be a kingdom of love, justice, holiness, salvation from sin, and the graces of divine life. He established the Church and the sacraments as the way by which the kingdom would be made available to us. Because this is a never-ending task until the Second Coming, all of us need to pray for the realization of the kingdom in our hearts and in the world. Jesus told Pilate that his kingdom is not of this world, meaning that it is not a political reality but a spiritual one that is meant to sanctify politics, economics, the arts and sciences, and every human heart.

Again at World Youth Day 2004, I met several young men from Bavaria on a subway train. One of them displayed his T-shirt and said, "Father, do you understand the words on my shirt, "*Ich Stehe fur Leben*?" "Yes," I replied, "it means 'I stand for life.'" Then they gave me a brochure that showed five young fathers holding their babies in their arms. Above the picture the words said, "Fatherhood is cool." On the back page, the fathers appeared again, gathered around an unborn child in the womb. The words accompanying the picture said, "We will always say yes to life." In that brief and warm encounter with the future, I saw God's kingdom taking shape in a new way.

Thy Will Be Done

In this petition, we face one of the most difficult aspects of prayer: acceptance of God's will. Jesus said he came to do the will of his Father. In his forty days in the desert, Jesus faced temptations by the devil to reject the Father's will. At Gethsemane, he sweat blood, so difficult was it to submit to the Father's will. Jesus wanted to experience the depths of human suffering and testing in the process of doing the Father's will. He gave us the words (accompanied by his example) to use: "Thy will be done." Jesus never promised us a rose garden. We face tremendous challenges to do God's will. But Jesus has won for us the power to do it. He became like us in every way but sin: "For because he himself has suffered and been tempted, he is able to help those who are tempted" (Heb 2:18).

In 1960, Adam Bujak, an acclaimed Polish photographer, did a series of photo essays of less-famous pilgrimages in Poland. His third photo essay is titled *The Celebration of the Sufferings of the Lord*. It shows a shrine in a remote farming area with 150,000 people gathered to reenact the Passion of Christ. The narrative accompanying the pictures of one particular chapel explains:

> *They gather around a life-sized wooden statue of Jesus, whose hands are chained to a pole and whose wound marks*

Gethsemane

can be seen. Pilgrims place candles around Jesus and talk to him as a friend. They stroke his face lovingly and tell him their problems. Some ask for cures or to be able to see or hear better. Others kiss his hands or his face and remain prostrate before him.

The pilgrims are not philosophizing about prayer. They are having face time with a Jesus who knows their pain. His capacity to accept God's will seeps into their hearts. As they love him, their problems are put in perspective, and they feel the peace of the will of God.

Give Us This Day Our Daily Bread

Christ's bread miracle was so important for the Gospel writers that they recorded it six times. On the one hand, it illustrates Christ's concern for our daily food needs. As the Word of God, through whom all things were made, Jesus gave us the harvests to satisfy our hunger. He was not like the man who was "so heavenly-minded he was no earthly good," but at the same time, Jesus ministered to the hungers of our souls.

St. John's Gospel connects the bread miracle with Christ's dialogue with the crowds about his forthcoming gift of Eucharist. At the Last Supper, Jesus provided us with the celebration of the Eucharist. The Apostles continued it in the Breaking of the Bread. For over 2,000 years, the Body of Christ (the Church) has been nourished daily by the Body of Christ (the Eucharist). No prayer surpasses the Mass. This liturgy of word and sacrament is the Church's "secret weapon" that assures her presence and effectiveness till Christ comes again. Jesus says, "Go ahead. Ask for manna — the food you need to live. And ask for Eucharist — the heavenly food for your spiritual growth." Give us our daily bread!

Archbishop Timothy Dolan tells the story of his meeting a young Chinese priest at Catholic University in Washington, DC. The priest had just received his doctorate in theology and was returning to China. He was invited to meet the Trustees, who questioned him thus:

"What will you do when you go home?"

"I am not sure."

"How will your bishop greet you?"

"He disappeared two months ago."

"Can you stay with your family?"

"My mom wants me to do that, but I won't, since it will endanger her."

"So what is left for you?"

"I will celebrate Mass every day and give people Communion wherever I can. That is my mission. That is God's will for me, to give people the Body and Blood of Christ."

Forgive Us Our Trespasses
As We Forgive Those Who Trespass Against Us

No one escapes the unpleasant instance of being injured, insulted, or disrespected by other human beings — and no one can boast of never causing pain in someone else. This universal experience of wounding and being wounded requires the healing balm of forgiveness. Such sins not only distress people; they also break or weaken our relationship with God. But God wants to reconcile us with himself. He loved us so much that he sent his Son to redeem us, to restore our relationship with him.

The whole life of Christ was a continual teaching: his silences, his miracles, his gestures, his prayer, his love for people, his special affection for the little and the poor, his acceptance of the total sacrifice on the Cross for the Redemption of the

world, and his Resurrection are the actualization of his word,
and the fulfillment of Revelation.

— *CCC* 561

The popularity of the Divine Mercy devotion is a testimony to the truth about the incredible mercy of God, who always wants to forgive us. On the Cross, he forgave the people who tormented him. He forgave the thief who asked to be remembered in the kingdom. Jesus gave us the Sacrament of Reconciliation on Easter night, when he breathed on the Apostles and gave them the Holy Spirit of reconciliation (cf. Jn 20:19-23). Jesus reminds us that we cannot be forgiven unless we forgive others. We must show mercy to obtain mercy "that flows like gentle rain from heaven above." Be slow to anger and swift to forgive.

In the autumn of 2006, a milkman entered the Amish school house in Nickel Mines, Pennsylvania. He pulled out a gun and chased out all the children except ten little girls. He shot them all, and then killed himself. Five girls died; five survived. The parents of the slain girls picked up their bodies, brought them home, removed the bloody clothes, and washed their bodies. Each family cleared a room of furniture except for chairs. Each girl was in a simple pine coffin that rested on a table. The family sat before it and mourned their loss. Then, the families went to the home of the widow of the man who killed their children. They told her that they forgave him for what he did. They consoled her for her own troubles and asked if they could hug her as a sign of reconciliation. The Amish parents buried their anger before their buried their children.

On the wall of the local firehouse dining room is a watercolor of the schoolyard painted by Elsie Beiler. Titled "Happier Days," it shows the Amish children playing without a care before the shooting. Five birds — that, some say, represent the children — circle the blue sky. Elsie felt it might comfort the parents in their struggle to live each day in forgiveness.

Lead Us Not Into Temptation

How odd of God to be thought of as tempting us to sin! Pope Benedict says that we should distinguish *testing* from *tempting*. God would never tempt us to sin, but he allows us to be tested. Our Lord assures us that he does not permit us to be tempted beyond our ability to resist it:

> *God is faithful, and he will not let you be tempted beyond your strength, but with the temptation will also provide the way of escape, that you may be able to endure it.*
> — 1 Cor 10:13

The most famous example of how a just man was tested so severely one wonders how he could endure it — without losing his mind or his faith — is Job. Yet he prayed:

> *"Naked I came from my mother's womb, and naked shall I return; the Lord gave, and the Lord has taken away; blessed be the name of the Lord."*
> *In all this Job did not sin or charge God with wrong.*
> — Job 1:21-22

St. Paul was tested by a thorn in the flesh. No one knows what it was, though scholars speculate about it regularly but inconclusively. So debilitating was it that three times he begged God to take it away. God refused; he told Paul that his grace was sufficient for him to endure it and not to lose faith. This petition asks us to face the inevitable trials that test our faith, patience, and hope with trust in God's plans for us and a belief that he would never put us to a test we cannot endure.

In the last month of his life, imprisoned in the Tower of London, St. Thomas More was visited by his wife Alice, daughter Margaret, and son-in-law Roper. For several years he had endured pressure from King Henry VIII, who wanted him to take the oath that acknowledged the validity of the king's divorce and remarriage, as well as his declaring himself head of the Church in England.

Margaret begged him to say the words of the oath but think otherwise in his heart. She said he had been as reasonable as any man could be. But More replied that he held his soul in his hands like water, and should he part his fingers, his soul would be lost. It was not just a matter of reason but love for God that made the difference.

Alice, too, said she could not understand why he was doing this. He wept and said he needed Alice's understanding. She could not understand, but she could tell the King that she had married the best man she ever knew.

This was the final test — More's last temptation from the people he loved most in the world. Then, the visit was over. More hugged his family and bade them goodbye. The next day, he was beheaded. He had passed God's test.

But Deliver Us From Evil

At some thoughts a man stands perplexed above all at the sight of human sin, and he wonders whether to combat it by force or by humble love. Always decide: "I will combat it by humble love." If you resolve that once and for all, you can conquer the whole world. Loving humility is a terrible force: it is the strongest of all things, and there is nothing else like it.
— FYODOR DOSTOEVSKY,
THE BROTHERS KARAMAZOV

In his humorous but dead serious book, *The Screwtape Letters*, C.S. Lewis describes how a devil named Uncle Screwtape tutors his nephew Wormwood in the arts of tempting people to do evil acts. Screwtape tells his nephew how to convince people that devils do not exist and that what people think is evil is actually not such a bad thing at all. He urges his youthful tempter to be content with getting his victim to perform little sins. It is the cumulative effect that separates the person from the enemy (Christ).

Lewis's book remains a relevant look at the moral atmosphere of contemporary life. Pope Benedict says much the same thing in a more philosophical way when he talks about the "dictatorship of relativism." It's a point of view that fudges the distinction

---

ST. CYPRIAN

Born in Carthage into a prominent pagan family around the year A.D. 200, Cyprian was trained as a lawyer and a polished public speaker. When he was thirty-five, he was converted to Christianity by an elderly priest named Caeceilian; eventually, he became a priest, then a bishop. Cyprian's Carthage was the center of Roman Africa's government, power, and wealth, presiding over what was called the "breadbasket" of the empire — endless fields of wheat, barley, and corn. Its educated class spoke Latin and adopted Latin culture.

Cyprian faced the first two persecutions mandated by imperial decree: Decius's in A.D. 250 and Valerian's in A.D. 257-258. He was strict but not inflexible with the Christians who gave up their faith during persecutions, giving them the possibility of forgiveness after a period of exemplary penance. He died as a martyr in 258.

Cyprian composed numerous treatises and letters, always linked to his pastoral ministry. In fact, the Church was his favorite subject. He never tires of repeating, "He who abandons the Chair of Peter, upon which the Church is founded, lives in the illusion that he still belongs to the Church . . . a unity that, as he says, finds its foundation in Peter and its perfect fulfillment in the Eucharist" (*The Unity of the Catholic Church* 4; Epistle 63:13).

St. Cyprian

between good and evil and claims we are beyond such categories. When we are lured into being "tolerant" and good-natured about evil, however, we lose a sense of the self-destructive power of that same evil. Our judgment becomes vague and milky.

The descent into evil goes something like this: The second sin is easier than the first. The more we sin, the less we think we are sinning. Soon, sin becomes strangely virtuous, and virtue appears to be unattractively bad. Eventually, we are hooked by sin and aggressively hostile to virtue. Apologists for evil tell us that God is basically angry and vengeful. Who wants such a religion? They never tell you that sin is its own punishment, for it enslaves the sinner.

This brief trip into the fog of modern morality makes Christ's deliverance from evil more necessary, yet difficult for many to grasp when they have been deceived by the "Father of Lies." The casual lifestyle is uncomfortable with absolute moral norms and brushes aside talk about sin and evil as remnants of a medieval mindset. It's an addiction to a dead end. The cure for this malaise is an encounter with the love and mercy of Christ, the Redeemer. When this cultural phase hits rock bottom, as it will eventually, the hope of the world — Jesus Christ, who delivers us from evil — will be rediscovered.

FOR REFLECTION

1. Which of the seven petitions of the *Our Father* touch you most deeply?
2. What are some of your life experiences that illustrate the *Our Father* that you could share with others?
3. How have you coped with the mystery of God's will for you?
4. How do you deal with forgiving others?
5. Why is the distinction between *testing* and *tempting* useful?

FOR CONTEMPLATION

All Christ did, all he taught, was the will of God:

- *Humility in our daily lives*
- *An unwavering faith*
- *Refusal to harm others*
- *Preferring nothing to Christ who preferred nothing to us*
- *Standing by his Cross with loyalty and courage whenever there is any conflict involving his honor and his name.*

— ST. CYPRIAN OF CARTHAGE,
COMMENTARY ON THE OUR FATHER, 13-15

Three

GOD'S PRAYER BOOK —
THE PSALMS

Yes indeed you are singing; you are singing clearly. I can hear you. But make sure that your life does not contradict your words. Sing with your voices, your hearts, your lips and your lives.

— ST. AUGUSTINE, *ON PSALM 96*

The Psalms are the greatest prayer book ever written: God's prayer book. In them, the Word of God becomes the prayer for every man and woman. The Psalms are prayers of praise and glory to God, as well as every other kind of prayer we need. No literature in existence is more penetrated with the songs of faith-filled praise to the glory of God than the Psalms that rise out of hearts committed to God with deep faith. It is good to know that the subtitle for the Book of Psalms is "The Praises."

Biblical faith centers on our surrender to a God who liberated Israel from slavery in Egypt, formed them as a covenant people at Sinai, and renewed his pledge of love through the Judges, Kings, Prophets, and Wisdom speakers.

Scriptural faith responds to this action of God in salvation history by a personal encounter with God in union with all God's people. For the Christian, this faith is a surrender to the Father, who saved us through his Son, Jesus Christ, in union with the Holy Spirit. It is personal as well as in communion with the Church, the Body of Christ.

The Psalms are songs rising from a community of faith, and this faith is never more evident than when the Church assembles for worship. In celebrating the Eucharist, the Church is visibly showing forth the faith of the community of believers. Psalms achieve their ultimate richness when sung from hearts with faith in God and in love with the Trinity. No one person exhausts the wealth of a psalm, nor does any psalm exhaust the faith of the believing community.

When Christians gather to sing the Psalms, they express the reality of the Church and proclaim their faith to the world. These "faith hymns" are not only a glad sound inviting an unbelieving world to become open to God; they are also a way in which the Holy Spirit forges the singers into a deeper communion with God. It is the will of Jesus that the attitudes of the Psalms will penetrate the hearts of the singers and move them to witness him to others.

The young Jesus himself sang psalms at home with his mother, Mary, and with the local community in the synagogue of Nazareth. He joined the melodies of the Psalms in pilgrimages to Jerusalem and in participating in worship in the Temple. His last act at the Last Supper, as he went to his Passion, was to sing a praise psalm, the great *Hallel* or *Halleluia* (Psalm 136).

Like faith itself, the Psalms stand on the plains of battle. They are not simply sweet sounds to charm the heavens, nor lusty emotional releases for the indiscriminate. Just as faith yearns to win the world for Christ, so the Psalms are its music motivating Christian witness. Psalm-singing is like the Cross — that is, a banner to be held high in the world for the unbeliever to see and ponder, and a flag in which the believer can see God and take heart.

In the book of Psalms there is profit for all, with healing power for our salvation. There is instruction from history, teaching from the law, prediction from prophecy, chastisement from denunciation, persuasion from moral preaching. All who read it may find the cure for their own individual failings. All with eyes to see can discover in it a complete gymnasium for the soul, a stadium for all the virtues, equipped for every kind of exercise; it is for each to choose the kind he judges best to help him gain the prize.

— St. Ambrose, *LH* Vol. III, p. 343

Where Do The Psalms Come From?

Many psalms arose from the mystic souls absorbed in prayer in the desert fastness that was the ordinary home of God's Jewish people during their nomadic years. Their desert and exile experiences were filled with silences, anxieties, and hopes that prompted prayers for help from God in their circumstances. The Psalms also sing of the joy of God's people when they marched in pilgrimage to the Holy City. For the crowning of their kings, for hailing the new year, for the merriment of marriage, they sang psalms. Psalms mingled with the sound of trumpets and the hoarse shouts of battle that Israel waged against her enemies.

To celebrate a meal, to comfort a lonely shepherd at night, to soothe the groans of the sick, there was always a ready psalm. To nurse the sting of backbiting and unfair decisions of law courts, to meet death bravely, to face the shame of a guilty conscience, Israel's faith produced a psalm. Psalms were the people's faith in the midst of life, death, war, and judgment. Psalms were a tapestry of action as well as contemplation. They could be sung alone on the mysterious heights of Mount Tabor — or, most often, in village synagogues and the Jerusalem Temple.

Mirror of God's Love Affair with Us

However, the Psalms are not only a chronicle of the colorful, ecstatic, and tragic aspects of the daily life of God's people; they are also a mirror of God's marvelous deeds in the history of his people. In a thousand ways, they sing of God's love affair with his people, his arguments with them, his affection and his reproaches, his warm mercy and his rebukes, his olive branch and his disappointments. They chant his promises and his demands, his fidelity and his silences, his ecstasy in giving himself to them and his regrets at their infidelity, his joy at their return to him and his glowing pleasure when they acknowledge him as their Shepherd.

The Psalms are just as much about God as they are about his people. Why is this so? It is because they are a living record of hundreds of years of the ups and downs of their divine-human relationship. Another way of thinking of their origin is to perceive them as a result of the religious experience of God.

This could be the exaltation of an individual feeling of God's presence and wanting to translate that into a prayer to be sung. Or, it could be the communal intimacy with God at worship or in a supreme historic moment, such as the song of Miriam after Israel crossed the Red Sea. Many of the Psalms have been composed for use in the liturgy. In the shadow of the Temple, fraternities of musicians gathered to compose melodies for the Psalms. These were worship songs, similar to Christian hymns that are created for liturgical use.

Who is the author of the Psalms? King David has long been considered to be the composer of the Psalms, and doubtless he wrote some of them. But studies about the dating of the Psalms, and a variety of historical references, conclude they were written over a number of centuries. Still, the powerful influence of David may have touched many composers after him. We always regard each psalm as a gift of God's revelation, appearing in the words of men and reflecting the language and culture of their times. The same Holy Spirit inspires both God's work and man's response. Jesus united these two aspects. In Jesus, the Psalms teach us how to pray.

For St. Augustine, the psalms were the record of the emotions of Christ and his members. Just as he had taken on human flesh, so Christ had, of his own free will, opened himself to human feeling. . . . When he turns to the psalms, Augustine will draw from them an immensely rich deposit of human emotions, for here was Christ speaking directly in the person of the passionate King David. The song of the desperate fugitive from the wrath of Saul is the inner story of the Passion. [Christ's] voice in the psalms, a voice singing happily, a voice groaning, a voice rejoicing in hope, sighing in its present state — we should know this voice thoroughly, feel it intimately, make it our own.

Augustine's sense of the bonds of human feeling... will seep into his preaching. In his sermons we begin to hear the songs of Africa. The sweet melody of a Psalm sung in the streets, the serenades, above all the rhythmic chant of the laborers in the fields.

— PETER BROWN, *AUGUSTINE OF HIPPO*
(UNIVERSITY OF CALIFORNIA PRESS, 1975), PP. 257-258

To Sing Is To Pray Twice*

St. Augustine says that he who sings prays twice. It is too bad that most people regard the Psalms as a text to be read silently. The Psalms are the songs of faith: war chants, victory songs, enthronement anthems, hymns about nature. There has been a revival in psalm singing, pioneered by the work of Frs. Joseph Gelineau and Lucien Deiss, French priest-musicians, and many other composers. The popularity of the guitar has an impact on the singing of psalms, not just because David used a stringed instrument but because it suits the vigorous rhythm of the words and the excitement of the situation.

---

*This section is quoted by the author from his book *Fr. McBride's Guide to the Bible*, OSV, 2004, pp. 91-93.

Israelite Poetry: The poetry of the Israelites differs from what most of us think poetry should be. There is no rhyme or rhythm in the sense we expect. Israelite poetry may be summed up by stating: never say anything once that you can say twice and even three times. The poetry of the Psalms is the rhythm and rhyme of *ideas*.

> *How long, O Lord? Will you be angry forever?*
> *Will your jealous wrath burn like fire?*
>
> — Ps 79:5

In this style of poetry, then, an idea is stated, then repeated with different shades of meaning. By way of exception, the second line sometimes simply completes a thought. At the same time, it must be said that in the Hebrew, there is also a poetic "beat" that accompanies the thought rhythms. Generally, this is not evident in the translations — but if you obtain a CD of psalms sung in Hebrew and accompanied by drums, you will experience this "beat."

Prayers of the Church: The Psalms hold a privileged position in the prayer life of the Church. They serve to show us how to pray. As part of sacred Scripture, the Psalms are God's revealed prayers composed by faith-drenched poets. The Church has chosen the Psalms as the centerpiece of the Liturgy of the Hours and given them an honored place in the Mass, especially in the Responsorial Psalm. For over fifteen centuries, monks and nuns in monasteries have accorded the Psalms a central place in their lives.

In singing the Psalms with the community, we are involved and, somehow, lifted up to God. The Psalms help us see that poetry and symbols in prayer can lead us to the throne of God. Finally, they remind us that all prayer reflects real life on earth and in heaven. The Psalms are rooted in the tears, smiles,

Pope St. Pius X

THE SONG OF THE CHURCH

St. Pius X loved the Psalms. He noted that from the beginning of the Church, the Psalms showed a wonderful power of fostering devotion among Christians. He reminded everyone that the Psalms play a conspicuous part in the Mass and the Liturgy of the Hours. Pius thought of them, as St. Basil did, as the "voice of the Church" that arises unceasingly up to the throne of God and of the Lamb.

In celebrating these prayers, the pope quotes St. Athanasius:

The psalms seem to me to be like a mirror, in which the person using them can see himself, and the stirrings of his own heart; he can recite them against the background of his own emotions.

To this, Pius adds a passage from St. Augustine's *Confessions*:

How I wept when I heard your hymns and canticles, being deeply moved by the sweet singing of your Church. Those voices flowed into my ears, truth filtered into my heart, and from my heart surged waves of devotion. Tears ran down, and I was happy in my tears.

Pius himself added:

Indeed, who could fail to be moved by those many passages in the psalms which set forth so profoundly the infinite majesty of God, his justice, goodness and mercy too deep for words . . . Who could fail to be roused to the same emotions by the prayers of thanksgiving to God for blessings received, by the petitions, so humble and confident . . . ? Who would not be fired with love as he looks on the likeness of Christ, the redeemer? His was the voice Augustine heard in every psalm, the voice of praise, of suffering, and of joyful expectation . . .

— Adapted from the Apostolic Constitution *Divino Afflatu* of Pope St Pius X, *LH* Vol. IV, pp. 1336-37 shouts, and noises of the world. Yet they carry us to the peace, repose, and echoes of heaven.

For Reflection

1. Read Psalm 23 slowly. It is known as the "Shepherd Psalm" and has thoughts about going to the next life as well as about the Eucharist in this life. Write about your feelings as you meditate on it.

2. Psalm 46:10 says, "Be still and know that I am God." Compare this advice with your daily tempo. Does it fit you? Are you too fast to slow down for God? What do you need to do?

3. How has our reflection on the Psalms opened you to praying them daily?

For Contemplation

Then hear, O gracious Savior,
accept the love we bring,
that we who know your favor
may serve you as our king;
and whether our tomorrows be filled with good or ill,
we'll triumph through our sorrows and rise to bless you still:
to marvel at your beauty
and glory in your ways,
and make our joyful duty
our sacrifice of praise.

Four

ADVICE ABOUT PRAYING . . .
From Augustine to the Lady Proba

For I know the plans I have for you, says the LORD, plans for welfare and not for evil, to give you a future and a hope. Then you will call upon me and come and pray to me, and I will hear you. You will seek me and find me; when you seek me with all your heart, I will be found by you, says the LORD . . .
— JER 29:11-14

As the Roman Empire began to crumble in the early fifth century, many worldly-wise noble families moved to safe havens in North Africa and Palestine. Constantine had made Christianity an established religion a century before, and many in the ruling class adopted the faith, including a number of prominent women who experienced God's call to a deeper relationship with him. Such was the case, for example, for a group of ladies who settled in Bethlehem to be guided by St. Jerome, who was engaged in a new translation of the Bible into Latin.

Lady Proba, matriarch of a powerful family and widow of the richest man in the empire, was the mother and aunt of consuls and had inherited vast agricultural holdings. From one of her estates in North Africa, she contacted Augustine and presented him with questions about her prayer life.

His letters to her contain a wisdom that endures for us today. From his advice to her, I have selected three of his themes that have a universal application to our own prayer and presented his wisdom in an imaginative dialogue based on a paraphrase of Augustine's Letter to Proba in the *Liturgy of the Hours* Vol. IV, pp. 407-413 and 425-430.

Lady Proba: I like to use a lot of words when I pray. I approach God with a number of petitions about my worries concerning my family, my exile, my health and my future. Yet Jesus says, "In praying do not babble like the pagans, who think they will be heard because of their many words. Do not be like them. Your Father knows what you need before you ask him" (Mt 5:7-8). Yes, but is there no value in words of petition?

Augustine: The psalmist says, "O God, you are my God, for you I long. My souls thirsts for you; my body pines for you like a dry, weary land without water" (Ps 63:2-3). The most important aspect of prayer is your desire for God, your yearning to be with him, your holy longing to be in his loving presence. The one thing to ask is the gift of being in a relationship with God. Our Lord does not need to know what we want; in fact he cannot fail to know it. Your prayers are meant to fire up your desire for God. The goal of prayers is to exercise your longing for God.

Think of it this way. God has an enormous gift of his love and happiness for you. To make that possible you need a capacity large enough to receive it. Daily prayer is like stretching your ability to take in what God wants you

---

Prayer stands before God as an honored ambassador. I speak of prayer, not words. It is the longing for God, love too deep for words, a gift not given by man but by God's grace. When the Lord gives this kind of prayer he gives us riches that cannot be taken away, heavenly food that satisfies the spirit. One who tastes this food is set on fire by an eternal longing for God: Your spirit burns as a fire with the utmost intensity.

— St. John Chrysostom, Homily 6, *On Prayer*

to have. The deeper your faith, the stronger your hope and the more fervent your love, the greater your desire for God will happen.

Set aside specific times each day for praying. Your words remind you of your various needs, and this is good. But beyond that, they should help you notice the progress you have made in your longing for God and motivate you to increase it. Turn your mind to prayer at appointed hours so you may overcome the tendency of your desire for God to get lukewarm due to your other concerns and occupations.

The words of prayer focus your attention on the desire for God so that the desire does not grow cold and even disappear unless it is constantly fired up. The more fervent your desire, the more worthy will be its outcome. St. Paul tells us to pray without ceasing. This means desiring God's life of happiness and asking him for it, since he alone can give it.

Lady Proba: I used to think that I should pray when I feel like it. It seemed to me that spontaneous prayer is more real. Now I am more open to what you mentioned about committing myself to appointed times for prayer, especially chanting the psalms in the morning and evening. I have attended such prayer at the local monastery and usually find it refreshing. I also set aside time for quiet prayer. I am still curious about the length of time that I need to pray. What is long and what is short? Does it matter?

Augustine: The Gospels tell us that Jesus sometimes spent a whole night in prayer and that he prayed at great length. These seem to be special times in comparison to regular times for prayer at the synagogue and during pilgrimages to the Temple. His long nights of prayer reflected his enduring filial relationship with his Father, typical of his eternal life, while his other regular but intermittent prayer was appropriate to his temporary life among us. In this, he gives you an example and guide for your own practice.

You may find yourself attracted to long prayer at times. This is good, so long as it does not interfere with your responsibilities. Still, such prayer should always include the yearning for God that I have mentioned repeatedly. Praying for a long time is not the same as multiplying words. Talking a lot is different from having a prayerful attitude.

I have heard that the monks in Egypt offer frequent prayers, that these are very short and hurled like swift spears into the presence of God. I think they consider watchful attention to God is so important that it should not be dulled by delays. They have learned by experience that when they are attentive to God, nothing should distract them while it lasts.

The ancient monks believed that certain verses of the Psalms released a special energy of the Holy Spirit. The same conviction was expressed in their typical use of Psalm verses as darts to indicate concise phrases from the Psalms which they could "let fly" almost like flaming arrows, for example, against temptations. John Cassian, a fourth-century writer, recalls that monks discovered the extraordinary power of the opening verse of Psalm 69: "God, come to my assistance; Lord, make haste to help me," which since then has introduced the Liturgy of the Hours.

— Pope John Paul II, Audience, April 4, 2001

The special value of prayer words and rituals is that they keep us in prayer training. If you only rely on the urge to pray, you will not likely continue to pray in the long run, for prayer is not an easy task. Going out to meet God requires an effort on your part. God requires this even though the effort does not cause contact with God. In his infinite freedom it is God who touches you and even supplies the grace to come to him.

Granting the role of words, I must add that in lengthy prayer you should come to God with a persistent fervor. This approach accomplishes more by sighs than words, more through tears than speech. After all, God accomplished the creation and the redemption through his Word and so listens to the pulse of the human heart, the deep sighs of those who seek him with all their might. My mother Monica sighed and wept over me for many years and sometimes wondered if God was listening. At one point, she was getting so discouraged she asked a bishop of there was any hope for me. He told her that such tears as she shed would win from God my conversion, and he was right.

Lady Proba: Another difficulty that nags me is the suitability of my petitions. How do I know whether what I pray for is right? How can I tell if it is good for my progress toward God or actually a vanity that comes more from my excessive self regard than for intimacy with our Lord? Where does scripture deal with my dilemma?

Augustine: St. Paul faced the same uncertainty you mention. Did he know what he should have prayed for when he begged God to take away his thorn in the flesh? Did he know that God had sent him this affliction to bruise him so he would not be puffed up with the marvel of the

St. Augustine

revelation he has received? He implored God three times to remove it and showed he did not know he was asking for the wrong thing. Eventually he heard the Lord's answer explaining why such a great man as he did not receive what he wanted. "My grace is sufficient for you, for power is made perfect in weakness (II Cor 12:9)."

We all have our pet requests and push God to grant them, forgetting Christ's advice to pray that God's will be done. That is Christ's own example at his agony in the garden. He asks that the cup of pain be passed from him, but he surrendered his will to the Father, "Father, if you are willing, take this cup away from me; still not my will but yours be done (Lk 22:42)." So if God does not grant your request, you should have no doubt at all that what

---

SING TO GOD WITH SONGS OF JOY

But how is this done? You must first understand that words cannot express the things that are sung by the heart. Take the case of people singing while harvesting in the fields or in the vineyards or when any other strenuous work is in progress. Although they begin by giving expression to their happiness in sung words, yet shortly there is a change. As if so happy that words can no longer express what they feel, they discard the restricting syllables. They burst out into a simple sound of joy, of jubilation. Such a cry of joy is a sound signifying that the heart is bringing to birth what it cannot utter in words.

Now, who is more worthy of such a cry of jubilation than God himself, whom all words fail to describe? If words will not serve, and yet you must not remain silent, what else can you do but cry out for joy? Your heart must rejoice beyond words, soaring into an immensity of gladness, unrestrained by syllabic bonds. *Sing to him with sounds of joy.*

— St. Augustine, Sermon on Psalm 32, *LH* Vol. IV, p. 1577

God wants is better for you than what you wanted for yourself.

Of all the things you can pray for, I urge you to beg God for happiness. It is popular to talk a lot about the meaning of happiness and what makes it happen. Yet real happiness that is most satisfying comes from God. Our prayer for happiness needs to proceed from love with a pure heart, a good conscience and a sincere faith. This happiness which God wants to give us is the beginning of the very life of heaven here on earth.

The immensity of this gift is so great that our minds cannot fully grasp for what we ask. We all have what I call an "instructed ignorance." We somehow sense God's gift of happiness but do not quite know the right way to ask for it. It eludes our logic. Here our power is in our humble weakness. Keep St. Paul's majestic words close to you:

> Likewise the Spirit helps us in our weakness; for we do not know how to pray as we ought, but the Spirit himself intercedes for us with sighs too deep for words. And he who searches the hearts of men know what is the mind of the Spirit, because the Spirit intercedes for the saints according to the will of God.
>
> — ROM 8:26-27

Your words, Lady Proba, cannot adequately express your desire for divine happiness; yet in your deepest moments you find that you desire it. If you were entirely ignorant of it, you would not yearn for it. You would not seek it with sighs, if you had it.

FOR REFLECTION

1. How would you answer Lady Proba's question about the use of words in personal, private prayer? Why do you think Augustine stresses the primacy of desire for God in prayer?
2. What has been your experience of the length of time you devote to prayer? What do you think is the connection between formal prayer such as Mass or Liturgy of the Hours and your personal, private prayer?
3. How have you understood Augustine's teaching on the right thing to pray for? What is St. Paul's view of the right intention in prayer?

FOR CONTEMPLATION

I always begin my prayer in silence, for it is in the silence of the heart that God speaks. God is the friend of silence. We need to listen to God because it's not what we say but what He says to us and through us. Prayer feeds the soul. As blood is to the body, so prayer is to the soul.

— BL. TERESA OF CALCUTTA

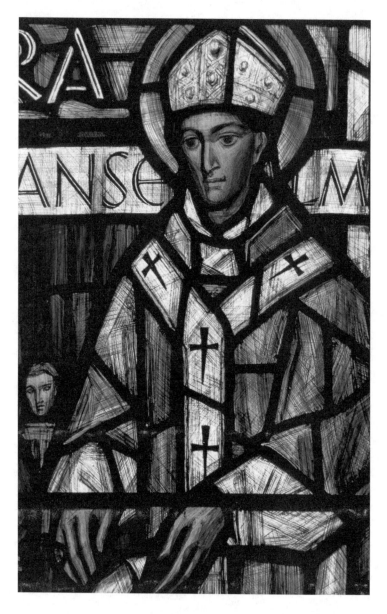

St. Anselm

Five

SOUL PRAYER...
According to St. Anselm (1033-1109)

Insignificant man, escape from your everyday business for a short while, hide for a moment from your restless thoughts. Break off from your cares and troubles and be less concerned about your tasks and labors. Make a little time for God and rest a while in him.

— ST. ANSELM, *LH* VOL. I, P. 184

Anselm was a mountain boy who grew up among the towering peaks of the Italian Alps, not far from the fabled Matterhorn. He recalled a childhood dream in which he imagined that God dwelt on those snowy heights. In his reverie, he climbed a mountain and soon met God, accompanied by a servant. He sat and talked with our Lord, telling him his name, where he lived, and what he wanted out of life, so that he would be ready to receive the "whitest bread in peace and communion." It was a Eucharistic picture of his yearning for the purest love of God.

After his mother's death, his home life deteriorated. Unable to get along with his father, he left home at age twenty-three and wandered around France for three years. Unfocused and untrained, he arrived at the Benedictine Abbey of Bec. Its abbot was Lanfranc, who had devoted much of his life defending the Real Presence of Jesus in the Blessed Sacrament against the denial of this truth of faith by Berengar of Tours.

Lanfranc — who had also started an abbey school for the liberal arts that attracted some of the brightest students of those days — recognized the raw genius of Anselm. He invited the young wanderer to join the abbey; for the next five years, he personally trained Anselm how to think with a disciplined mind and use the tools of the new learning. He had enough confidence in Anselm's talent to install him as the prior of the community. When Lanfranc was chosen Archbishop of Canterbury, he was succeeded by Anselm as the new Abbot of Bec.

During his thirty-three years at Bec, Anselm was shaped spiritually, morally, and intellectually by the Rule of St. Benedict and the liturgical and communal life of the monks, as well as by the formation of his mind through the training he received from Lanfranc. He wrote three works by which he left his mark on history: *Prayers and Meditations*; the *Monologion*; and the *Proslogion*.

Obviously, his book on prayer deals directly with spirituality, but his other two books — though more focused on theology and philosophy — consistently illumined the role of the soul in prayer. Perhaps one way of appreciating his contribution to our prayer life today is to summarize his major thoughts in four of his key teachings.

1. Maintain the primacy of faith.

He was first of all a monk, but he used his singular intellectual gifts to enhance his monastic commitment. He never forgot St. Benedict's motto, *Pax et Obedientia* (Peace and Obedience). Anselm believed that obedience was more than a mechanical submission to the details of monastic rules enforced by a superior; it was an "obedience of faith," responding to God's call to union with him through a life treasured by centuries of monks living vitally in God's presence. The peace of the monastery was the immediate outcome of obedient faith.

The spiritual life is a pilgrimage of faith. When faith is practiced as constantly hearing God's call and noticing God's presence in the call, then the stress of community and the threat of mere conformity are surmounted.

2. Adopt a faith that seeks understanding.

Anselm's particular genius was to connect faith and reason in the life of prayer. The dawn of the high Middle Ages, of which he was an early sentinel, would be called the Culture of Faith. Gothic cathedrals hovered over the landscape. Monastery towns appeared as enclaves of Christian devotion. A kind of mystical aura penetrated the medieval world. Saints' festivals were as common as the cycle of the seasons. An idealism animated by spirituality was expected — and practiced.

Anselm fully supported the adventure of faith so characteristic of his culture. But he also prized God's gift of reason in the drama of faith. His unique contribution to spirituality involved the application of reason to the mystery of the relationship of the soul to God. Clearly, faith was a gift, but so was reason. He coined the adage that faith spurs the use of reason: *Credo ut intelligam* (I believe, that I may understand). He said that our intelligence should be used not to change the content of divine teachings, but to understand them more clearly and see how they apply to our relationship with God.

Anselm found that sometimes thinking about the nature of God disposed him to receive an insight from God during prayer: His biographer, Eadmer, recalls this fact.

> One night during Matins [Office of Readings] the grace of God shone in his heart, the whole matter became clear to his mind, and a great joy and jubilation filled his whole being... "Thank you, good Lord," he exclaimed, "for by your gift I first believed, and now by your illumination I understand."
> — EADMER, *LIFE OF ANSELM*, I, XIX

In his view, the treasure of our reason helps us to make faith more active in the progress of our souls on the way to God. A lively reason works best when it urges our hearts to receive the gift of faith more joyfully. By making reason one of faith's best friends, we bring to our souls a link that ties human nature to our participation in the life of God more dynamically.

3. Believe, that you may understand.

Today, when so many people look at the words of the Apostles' Creed or the Nicene Creed, they treat the truths about God in a cool, detached manner. When deciding what the words mean, such as stating that Christ is "God from God, one in being with the Father," the words are treated as abstract statements that need to be unraveled as though they were math formulas. Anselm would never make that mistake. He imagined how God would advise us:

> *"If you want to know what that text means, begin with an act of faith. Pray the words, don't just think about them as a puzzle. Get in touch with me, the living God who in my love is sharing this intimate truth about the inner life between me and my Son. I am inviting your soul into the sanctuary of the Trinity.*
>
> *"Why do you think I have given you my Holy Spirit if not to have a guide to this holy ground? Why have I given you the gift of faith at your Baptism and enlarged it in Communion and the other sacraments? Believe, that you may understand. When you bring your gift of intelligence, never misuse it by making it a distant observer of my divine life, but rather come as my beloved who is in a relationship with me."*

INTERPRETING THE BIBLE

In our time, Anselm would advise us to use the same approach when studying the Bible. We should come to Scripture with an attitude of faith and reverence, because we meet God in these holy pages. At every liturgy, after the reading of Scripture, we hear the reader say, "The Word of the Lord." Our response is, "Thanks be to God." The dialogue is a matter of faith, pure and simple.

When we study Scripture, we may use commentaries to obtain interpretations, dictionaries to explain strange words, atlases to locate biblical sites on maps of Palestine, differing translations to obtain a richer grasp of the texts, or homilies from the Fathers of the Church to inspire us through God's Word. Now, if we listen to Anselm for his advice on what to do, he will immediately tell us:

Believe what you read is God's Word for your life, hope, joy and love. Get involved in the text as if it were a living conversation between you and God. Cherish the lines as messages from an all loving and saving God.

Yes, you will find puzzling passages and difficult sentences and strange stories. Sometimes you will try to sort out the meanings from a purely logical standpoint or even from a detached, lofty perspective. While there is true value in this rational approach, you should never lose the grip of faith when pondering puzzling lines. Stay firmly in the shadow of God's wings. Let you soul cling to Christ. Let the Holy Spirit hold you by that hand. You will discover that believing in God is the surest path to understanding the Word of God. The great Fathers of the Church sat for hours with the Bible open on their laps, its words catching their eyes and its voice speaking to their hearts. They were in communion with God who flooded their intelligence with the divine poetry that wove itself into their incomparable interpretations that still move our souls centuries later.

When reading Gospels, allow your soul to long for God, tell the Lord that you thirst for his palpable presence, that even your body yearns for him as though it were a dry land without water. This is the prompting of faith. This is the fervent believing that leads to understanding. The mind needs illumination of faith to start the motors of logic and reasoning that will bring the gaze on the Lord's glory in the sanctuary.

In other words, Anselm teaches us that God is only too willing to flood our minds with understanding of his revelation — not just what he taught us, but what it means. The fact that library shelves groan with hundreds of faith-filled masterpieces, dating from apostolic times to the present, is incontestable testimony to this truth. But in our secular times, many of us are tone-deaf to this old teaching of Anselm. Too often we reverse his axiom, putting understanding first and faith second. This weakens the role of faith and imperils authentic understanding of God's passionate appeals to our hearts.

The result is that we start with an invisible wall between us and God. We break the link between reason and faith, and so reduce our understanding of creeds, Scripture, and Church teachings to what makes sense to us apart from a relationship with God. Such an approach leaves us destitute, because we treat relationship from an analytic point of view instead of the perspective of love. In fact, the idea of relationship is actually left out of the equation — which is sad, because God begins his approach to us with love, not as if observing us through the lens of a microscope.

4. Make your prayer personal.

How did Anselm figure all this out? What was his secret? Was his intelligence the key? Of course, his being very bright helped — but only when his faith was living, active, and on fire. He is best remembered for his theological works, but his influential writings in the Middle Ages were about prayer. He struck a chord in a culture that both valued objective truth but was also ready for the personal, the subjective, and, yes, the emotional dimension. The best way to translate his axiom, "I believe, that I may understand," is found in his book, *Prayers and Meditations.*

As a Benedictine monk, he spent thirty-three years in the monastic choir, singing the Psalms and canticles of the Bible in the Divine Office, along with a prayerful listening to readings from the Old and New Testament and from homilies from the Fathers of the Church. All this praise of God culminated in the celebration of the Eucharist. There is no doubt that this being drenched by the Word of God and the Blessed Sacrament was a transforming power in his life.

Yet, Anselm felt something was missing. Despite all that magnificent prayer, he believed that he, and others, needed something more. He would never question the value of community prayer and worship: how else, he asked himself, could the love of God shape his mind, heart, and even subconscious, especially since so many of the Psalms were memorized? But God led him to something more. God prompted him to write personal prayers. Even in the midst of his theological writings, God moved him to break into personal prayer, such as in the following text:

> Lord, my God, teach my heart where and how to seek you,
> where and how to find you.
> Lord, if you are not here,
> where shall I look for you in your absence?
> Yet if you are everywhere,
> why do I not see you when you are present?
> But surely you dwell in "light inaccessible."
> And where is light inaccessible?
> How shall I approach light inaccessible?
> Or who will lead me and bring me into it that I may see you
> there?
> And then by what signs and under what forms shall I seek
> you?
>
> — *Proslogian*, Chapter 1

His prayer is personal, alive, and accessible. He is talking out loud to God, very much as the psalmists did so often. In the manner of St. Augustine's *Confessions*, he publicly spoke to God about their relationship. In the middle of a theological masterpiece, he is unashamed to stop and complain to God about seeking his face and somehow not finding it. To those of us today who read about Blessed Mother Teresa's long years of dryness in prayer, these words ring a bell.

Anselm's written personal prayers are important for us in our need for what is popularly called devotional prayer. It is no mistake that people of faith seek prayer forms that enliven their personal relationship with God. We certainly need ritual and established forms of prayer, such as the Liturgy of the Hours and the Eucharist. But we also find that popular piety helps us participate in the liturgy more effectively and strengthens our relating to God in a simple, down-to-earth manner.

Anselm's written prayers set a style for such books in the Middle Ages. He tells his readers to feel free and easy with his prayers. These are not ritual prayers that must be recited in a precise, orderly manner. These are prayers that one can use informally and with no sense of uncalled-for restraint, but rather suited to a quiet time in which the soul can freely pick out a passage here and there that matches the need of the hour. Following is Anselm's own introduction to his prayers:

> *The purpose of the prayers and meditations that follow is to stir up the mind of the reader to the love or fear of God, or to self examination. They are not to be read in a turmoil, but quietly, not skimmed or hurried through, but taken a little at a time with deep and thoughtful meditation.*
>
> *The reader should not trouble about reading the whole of any of them, but only as much as, by God's help, one finds useful in stirring up the soul to pray, or as much as one likes.*

Nor is it necessary always to begin at the beginning, but wherever one pleases.

With this in mind the sections are divided into paragraphs so that the reader can begin and leave off wherever one chooses; in this way, one will not get bored with too much material but will be able to ponder more deeply these things that will make him want to pray.

— *PRAYERS AND MEDITATIONS*, P. 89

Never forget that Anselm related enthusiastically to God despite being a busy abbot of a great monastery — leading the monks, supervising finances, meeting visiting politicians, businessmen, professors, artists, and musicians — and, probably, settling local disputes in the town around Bec. Such distractions multiplied when he was named Archbishop of Canterbury, where he disputed the King's interference in issues that were strictly Church matters. The stormy relationship with the King resulted in Anselm's being exiled. These upsets, on top of his shepherd's concern for God's people, would seem to be enough to put prayer on hold until he could recover his inner calm. But the opposite was true, for his inner fire was further warmed by

FIND GOD BY LOVE —
LOVE GOD IN THE FINDING

Teach me, Lord, to seek you and when I seek you, show yourself to me, for I cannot seek you unless you teach me, nor can I find you unless you show yourself to me.

> Let me seek you in desiring you,
> And desire you in seeking you,
> Find you in loving you,
> And love you in finding you.

— St. Anselm, *Proslogian*, Chapter 1

God's loving attention to the soul prayer of one of his greatest friends in all of Christendom.

Anselm believed in his beloved Lord.

Anselm understood his mysterious Master.

FOR REFLECTION

1. In praying, why should we hide for a time from our restless thoughts? How can we make a little time for God and rest in him? What is the value of escaping from your everyday business to spend time with God?

2. When you hear Anselm's advice to "Believe, that you may understand," how does this fit your view of the relationship of faith and reason? Why is the primacy of a faith relationship with God essential for understanding what God reveals to us about his life and love?

3. What ways have you discovered to help you read the Bible in a prayerful manner, with a vivid sense of conversing with God in these holy pages?

FOR CONTEMPLATION

Never will we leave you, Lord;
you will fill us with your life,
and we will call on your name.
Remember us, Lord, because of the love you have for your
   people.
Show us your face and we shall be saved.
   — RESPONSORY, ST. ANSELM; *LH* VOL. I, PP. 185-186

Six

THE WOMAN WHO TALKED
WITH GOD
St. Catherine of Siena
(1347-1380)

Charles Dickens wrote that history is a record of the "best of times and the worst of times." Historian Barbara Tuchman judged that the calamitous fourteenth century was the worst of times, a period afflicted by the Black Plague, the Hundred Years' War, and the Avignon Papacy. The plague killed over a third of Europe's population. The war was brutal and a scourge to thousands. The popes resided in Avignon for seventy years, sinking progressively more deeply under the influence of the French monarchy and losing their spiritual influence over the wider Church.

This was the woeful world into which Catherine of Siena was born, the twenty-fifth child of her family. She proved to be a precocious child, strong-willed and spiritually inclined. At the age of sixteen, she became a member of the Third Order of St. Dominic. This enabled her to follow many of the rules of cloistered nuns while wearing a modified habit and living as a laywoman in the world.

The Christian culture of the Middle Ages witnessed a growth of mysticism as seen in the lives of Hildegarde of Bingen, Julian of Norwich, Thomas à Kempis, and Bernard of Clairvaux. Like Bernard, Catherine loved the Old Testament "Song of Songs." She yearned to be fixed in perfect faith, so she could become an instrument of the salvation of souls. Catherine related that, in fact, Jesus took her for his bride;

that Christ confirmed her betrothal to him through a series of spiritual communications. Strongly drawn to meditation, she eventually began to have mystical experiences characterized by trances and raptures, especially after receiving Communion. She treated these happenings as gifts of love from God. Closely allied to her ecstatic experiences were acts of deprivation of sleep, food, and comfort.

Unlike many mystics, however, Catherine balanced contemplation and action; her testimony about her inner life never cut her off from involvement in everyday life, charitable endeavors, and deep involvement in the affairs of Church and state. For her, there seemed to be little or no tension or conflict between contemplation and action, as is so frequently described in the Martha-Mary story recounted in the Gospels. Catherine was blessed with a seamless garment of both.

The mystic Catherine was an outgoing person who visited the prisons, volunteered long hours at the hospital, and did what she could to relieve the sufferings of the poor. She had a special interest in prisoners about to be beheaded — praying with them at the execution site, urging them to seek forgiveness from God, and doing what she could to help them through the ordeal.

When the plague of 1374 struck Siena, Catherine actively ministered to the victims, including ten members of her family. Blessed with abundant native common sense and a warmhearted sympathy, she was frequently approached for spiritual direction. She dispensed such advice volubly and generously.

Since many of her mystical trances occurred in church, she naturally became the subject of much attention, gossip, and curiosity in Siena. Her good works won respect, since she dealt with so many difficult cases. But it was her mystical life that awakened the greatest interest in her, with reactions that ranged from skepticism, irreverence, hostility, and incredulity to belief, awe, and a desire to be nearer to God.

Spiritual Director

By the time she was twenty-three, she was surrounded by a group of spiritually-minded people of all ages and walks of life who looked to her as a guide for meditation, prayer, and personal moral improvement. This utterly self-confident young woman accepted this responsibility as a spiritual leader, referring to her followers as her "family" — her "children." With no apparent embarrassment, they returned the compliment and called her *Mamma.*

However, since she had no wealth, social standing, or any other public source for her authority, she needed some official backing — an affirmation she received from the Dominican Order. The Dominican priest, Raymond of Capua, served as her confessor, as well as a validator of her mission by his constant presence. He supervised the "secretarial pool" that wrote out the enormous amount of dictation which Catherine delivered. Raymond himself did some of the secretarial work, sometimes falling asleep in the wake of her voluminous outpourings.

In her young adulthood, she focused on prayer and charitable endeavors, but in the last eight years of her life, Jesus turned her attention to public affairs. Even as she remained in the shadow of God's wings, she received many letters from Christian kings, princes, and other leaders, seeking her advice about prayer or guidance for their complex problems. Closest to her heart, however, was the issue of the Avignon papacy. She was convinced that the pope must return to Rome and extricate himself from the financial bondage and political pressures exercised on him by the French government.

Changing the Pope's Mind

Her opportunity to do something about this problem arose when the government of Florence chose her to go to Avignon to settle a dispute between the prince and the Pope. She accepted the commission readily, believing she could also convince the Pope to return to Rome. She rented an apartment near the papal palace and went to the papal court nearly every day for four months. There, she negotiated peace between Florence and Avignon — then spent the subsequent months lobbying Pope Gregory XI to go back to Rome.

With no hint of shyness nor the slightest evidence of intimidation, she used a forthright approach with the Pope — sometimes calling him *Dolce Babbo Mio* (My Sweet Daddy). But that tender term didn't mean her message was meek or docile. On the contrary — she used dozens of arguments to plead her case with Gregory,

"Be a man, Holy Father!" she would plead. "Arise! Don't be negligent! Begin the reform of the Church through appointing worthy priests. Make peace in Italy, not by military force, but by pardon and mercy. Return to Rome, not with swords and soldiers, but with the Cross and the Blessed Lamb. Oh, Holy Father! Peace, for the love of God!"

There probably never have been papal audiences like these, before or since.

Theologians tried to discredit Catherine but emerged from meeting with her in several twelve-hour sessions, drawn, tired, exhausted — and converted. The totally confident Catherine, bolstered by her intense union with God, sat easily in the center of power, stared down the mighty, and changed the mind of Pope Gregory. He finally surrendered to her when she asserted, "Who knows God's will so well as Your Holiness? When you were a cardinal, you vowed that the papacy should be returned to Rome."

That bold statement shook him deeply, as he *had*, indeed, made such a personal vow to himself should he ever become Pope — a vow he had never told a living soul. Now this young woman before him knew his secret. Through his faithful servant, Catherine, God had touched his conscience. True to his word, Pope Gregory made the decision to move back to Rome and end what history called the "Babylonian captivity of the Popes," a reference drawn from the Old Testament history of the seventy years when the Jewish people lived as captives in Babylon.

The French king and his diplomats strove to persuade Gregory to stay, but he dismissed all arguments. He did worry about his health and grew nervous when he heard that a storm had ruined several papal ships. At the last moment, in a scene worthy of a Verdi opera, the Pope's father threw himself on the ground before his august son and begged him to stay, but Gregory tenderly lifted him up and quietly told him this was the will of God. Then Pope Gregory sailed for Rome.

What Florentine and Roman diplomats had been unable to persuade Pope Gregory to do, Catherine achieved by the power of her many hours of prayer each day in the chapel and the daily moral and spiritual witness of her life in the midst of the papal court.

As the pope traveled by sea, Catherine took the overland route back to Siena — now, an international celebrity, mobbed by curious and admiring crowds in town after town. In her own mind, she had more important things to do than to cope with the burdens of fame. Her experiences of the evils of Avignon had released a flood of reflections from God in her mind that required recording. She would be keeping her secretaries well occupied.

Back in Siena, she began dictating her Avignon memoirs, those chapters of her *Dialogues* that dealt with the sins of some priests, but also those who were "angels appointed by God's burning love to be lamps in the mystic body of the Church." Moved by the Spirit, she recorded comments such as the following:

> "[God speaks.] How humbly the priests governed and communicated with their subjects. With what hope and lively faith they generously gave out the Church's possessions to the poor. They fulfilled to the utmost their obligation to divide their temporal goods to meet their own needs and those of the poor and the Church. They set nothing aside, and after their death there was no great estate to settle. In fact some of them left the Church in debt for the sake of the poor, all because of their generous charity and their trust in my providence. They were not afraid so they were confident they would lack nothing, either spiritually or temporally."
>
> — *The Dialogue* (Paulist Press), p. 226

Catherine died in her thirty-third year, on the Sunday before the feast of the Ascension. Her last words were full of self-reproach that she had not loved as deeply as she knew was possible, but no one agreed with her. Their *Mamma* had loved God and others more than any of them believed possible. The Church concurred by canonizing her a saint in 1461 and making her a co-patron of Italy, along with St. Francis of Assisi, in 1939. Pope Paul VI named her a Doctor of the Church on October 4, 1970. Images of Catherine from the earliest days pictured her holding a book — a sure sign that she was informally known as a Doctor of the Church.

Speaking of images, there is an austere statue of Catherine on Rome's Via Della Conciliazione, the grand avenue leading up to St. Peter's. The statue faces the avenue, but her head is turned to the basilica. Her eyes are still on the popes.

THE INTERPLAY OF KNOWLEDGE AND LOVE

At the beginning of the *Dialogue,* Catherine establishes a principle of prayer that governs her relationship with God. Speaking of herself, she wrote:

> *I have for sometime exercised myself in virtue and have become accustomed to dwelling in the cell of self knowledge in order to know better God's goodness toward me since knowledge follows love. And loving I seek to pursue truth and clothe myself in it.*

— *Dialogue,* 1

In our scientific age, we argue that knowledge opens us to truth, while romantic films dramatize the axiom, "To know me is to love me." But Catherine's experience in prayer told her that love of God leads to knowing him. Love also leads to knowing truths about God. Finally, love reveals to her that God is truth. Catherine's starting point in prayer is love of God; love brings her into a personal relationship with God.

Of course, some kind of knowledge comes first. We cannot love what we do not know. In Catherine's case, God began the relationship, flooding her with his loving presence and gifts of prayer, inviting her to a divine-human experience of love that moved her to ecstasy at a young age. From then on, the love of God was the driving force in her life. She does not seem to think that she was so much learning truths *about* God as perceiving God as living Truth, as well as her beloved Lord.

Her abiding lesson of prayer for us is the plea to approach God with gratitude for the love he gives us and emphasize our desire to love him in return. We will continue to learn truths about God from Scripture, liturgy, moral laws, Church history, theology, and catechesis. When refined by our loving union with God in prayer, this knowledge supports what we will experience in loving God. We will experience what Jesus said to the apostles, "I am the way, the truth and the life" (Jn 14:6). There is an interplay between love and truth: truth leads us to God, and love leads us to believe and understand truth.

St. Catherine of Siena

DO FOR YOUR NEIGHBOR WHAT YOU CANNOT DO FOR ME.

From a dialogue in which God is speaking to Catherine:

I ask you to love me with the same love with which I love you. But for me you cannot do this, for I love you without being loved. Whatever love you have for me you owe me, so you love me not gratuitously but out of duty, while I do not love you out of duty but gratuitously. So you cannot give me the kind of love that I ask of you. This is why I have put you among your neighbors, so that you can do for them what you cannot do for me — that is, love them without any concern for thanks and without looking for any profit for yourself. And whatever you do for them I will consider done for me.

So your love should be sincere. You should love your neighbor with the same love you have for me. Do you know when your spiritual love is not perfect? If you are distressed when it seems that those you love are not returning your love or not loving you as much as you think you love them. Or if you are distressed when it seems to you that you are being deprived of their company or comfort, or that they love someone else more than you.

Loving me is like a vessel that you fill at a fountain. If you remove it from the fountain to drink, the vessel is soon empty. But if you hold your vessel in the fountain while you drink, it will not get empty. Indeed it will always be full. If your love for me and for your neighbors is still imperfect you have been drinking from your vessel outside the fountain.

— From the *Dialogues*, with an introduction and translation by Susan Noffke (Mahwah, NJ: Paulist Press, 1980)

Prayer

Eternal Trinity, Godhead, mystery deep as the sea, you could give me no greater gift than the gift of yourself. For you are a fire ever burning and never consumed, which itself consumes all selfish love that fills my being. Yes, you are a fire that takes away the coldness, illuminates the mind with its light and causes me to know your truth . . . I know that you are beauty and wisdom itself. The food of angels, you gave yourself to man in the fire of your love.

You are the garment which covers our nakedness, and in our hunger you are a satisfying food, for you are sweetness and in you there is no taste of bitterness. O triune God!

Christ responds:

My sister and my beloved, open yourself to me,
you are a coheir of my kingdom
and you have understood the hidden mysteries of my truth.
You are enriched with the gift of my Spirit,
cleansed of all sin by the shedding of my blood, alleluia.
Go forth from the quiet of contemplation
and courageously bear witness to my truth.
— Adapted from *LH* Vol. II, p. 1795

For Reflection

1. Why is it possible for people with great gifts of prayer to be able to engage in affairs of state and public life? How can a contemplative and mystic get involved in such activity as Catherine did?

2. How do you react to Catherine's boldness in her words of Pope Gregory XI? What was there about her forthrightness that the Pope found irresistible?

3. How do you account for the extraordinary energies people of deep prayer often demonstrate in their lives?

FOR CONTEMPLATION

Eternal Father, you have given me a share in your power and wisdom that Christ claims as his own. Your Holy Spirit has given me the desire to love you. You are my Creator, eternal Trinity, and I am your creature. You have made of me a new creation in the blood of your Son, and I know that you are moved with love at the beauty of your creation, for you have enlightened me.

— ST. CATHERINE OF SIENA

Seven

A Warrior's Way of Prayer
St. Ignatius of Loyola
(1491-1556)

Born in the castle of Loyola, Spain, Ignatius was one of thirteen children. Raised to be a soldier and receiving little schooling, he displayed no interest in religion. An eager reader of romantic stories about courageous knights, he chose the wife of King Ferdinand as his "Queen of Hearts" at the time of his investiture as a knight. He wore her colors and dreamed of winning a lace handkerchief from her as a tournament prize. His secret love for her, however, did not stop him from other romances — and the brawls that often characterize a soldier's life.

Ignatius spent four years of active duty in Pamplona until his leg was shattered by a cannonball during a battle with the French. The field surgeon set his bones and sent him home. Unfortunately, the bones were wrongly aligned, so they had to be re-broken and reset. The second operation proved to be more incompetent than the first; a stump of bone stuck out, so he had to endure a third operation in which the leg was finally straightened out but left a little shorter than his other leg. He spent frustrating weeks of pain as a stretching device secured his injured leg.

As the boring months of convalescence wore on, Ignatius asked for some books on chivalry to distract him, but the only books in the library were a life of Christ and a collection of lives of the saints. At the start, his militant tastes did not take to these apparently irrelevant stories. As time wore on, though — to his surprise — the lives of the saints proved to be as dramatic as the tales of courageous knights, and the figures of Christ and

Mary affected him deeply, leading to his religious conversion. In his mind, Ignatius visualized the biggest war of all: Christianity versus Islam. He would become a spiritual soldier, go to Jerusalem, and liberate Christianity from the Moslems. He resolved to be a soldier of Jesus and Mary until his death.

SPIRITUAL TRANSFORMATION AT MANRESA

Traditionally, knights of old would visit the Benedictine Abbey of Montserrat and pray before the shrine of the Virgin there before undertaking their exploits. Ignatius decided to go there as a pilgrim to begin his spiritual "knighthood." Arriving at the

---

IMPACT OF THE LIVES OF SAINTS

While reading the life of Christ or the lives of the saints, he would reflect and reason with himself: "What if I should do what Saint Francis or Saint Dominic did?" In this way he let his mind dwell on many thoughts; they lasted a while until other things took their place. Then those vain and worldly images would come into his mind and remain a long time. This sequence of thoughts persisted with him for a long time.

But there was a difference. When Ignatius reflected on worldly thoughts, he felt intense pleasure; but when he gave them up out of weariness, he felt dry and depressed. Yet when he thought of living the rigorous sort of life the saints had lived, he not only experienced pleasure when he actually thought about it, but even after he dismissed these thoughts, he still experienced great joy. . . . [h]e began to marvel at the difference. Thoughts of one kind left him sad, the other kind filled him with joy. And this was the first time he applied a process of reasoning to his religious experience. Later on, when he began to formulate his spiritual exercises, he used this experience as an illustration to explain the doctrine he taught his disciples on the discernment of spirits.

— Adapted from *The Life of St. Ignatius*
by Luis Gonzalez, *LH* Vol. III, 1565-66

---

monastery, Ignatius gave away his fine clothes, donned a beggar's robe, and spent the night before the shrine of the Mother of God, pledging vows of poverty and chastity to her.

After a few more days of prayer, he felt ready to go to Jerusalem and fulfill his dream. On his way, he stopped at the village of Manresa and stayed the night in a cave. That evening, a new awareness dawned on him: he had not begun to match or surpass the saints in their ascetic preparation for such a mission. He canceled his immediate plans for Jerusalem and embarked on a year-long bout of brutal self-deprivations. Determined to crush his male vanity, he stopped washing, cutting, or combing his hair. He wouldn't cut his nails or bathe himself. He gave up meat, begged what little food he ate, scourged himself, slept little, and prayed for long hours.

In fact, he almost killed himself, and might have died, but for a sympathetic woman who took him home and nursed him back to health. She persuaded him to move to the local Dominican monastery, where a watchful community could curb his extremism, but Ignatius felt he had not yet crushed the inner demons that tormented him and resumed his self-scourging.

In his darkest hour, finally, the turnaround began. He had visions of Christ and Mary that comforted him. Inner peace replaced his anxieties, and a sense of hope drove away the demons that plagued him during his year of trial at Manresa. Virtually reborn, he was intoxicated with God's presence and captured the meaning of his soul battle in the epic document of spiritual guidance, *The Spiritual Exercises.*

Feeling thoroughly prepared at last to evangelize the Moslems, he traveled to Jerusalem — only to face disillusionment. The Moslem rulers allowed Christians to visit as pilgrims but strictly forbade conversion efforts. The local Franciscan provincial, mandated to keep peace in the Holy City, advised the dispirited Ignatius to go home.

Having brought his body and soul under control, Ignatius decided to improve his mind. This thirty-three-year-old war veteran and newly honed man of prayer began a ten-year-long series of studies at Alcala, Salamanca, and Paris. He also had the itch to teach; when he gathered a group of women around him for seminars on asceticism, however, their husbands were not amused. They thrashed him and threatened him with more if he did not stop.

He moved on and, this time, worked with poor women and prostitutes. A few of them started having trances, drawing the attention of the Inquisition to what Ignatius was doing. They tried him and put him in jail until he convinced them that he was completely orthodox; at that point, they released him but forbade him to teach. In Salamanca, he went through the same cycle of teaching, Inquisition, imprisonment, and acquittal, and had enough. He saw no future in Spain, so he departed for Paris.

The Spiritual Exercises

While he was completing his work on a master's degree in Paris, Ignatius attracted a group of men who would become a nucleus of his new religious order — the Society of Jesus (or, the Jesuits, as they would become more popularly known). Chief among his new friends were Pierre Favre and Francis Xavier, the latter man coming from Pamplona, where Ignatius had served as a soldier.

Ignatius put them through the paces of his Spiritual Exercises, a methodical, systematic route to prayer. It was flexible enough for use in the noisy, distracting, complicated, manmade rhythms of the great cities of the world, where the Jesuits were often destined to minister. The express purpose of Ignatius was to bring his men to experience a spiritual conversion through a carefully planned series of meditations.

St. Francis Xavier

They began with self-analysis, examining their selfishness, lust, avarice, and other forms of human sinfulness that needed to be overcome while embarking on the journey to holiness. They needed to recognize what kind of personal change they required.

Next, Ignatius led them to realize that commitment to Christ makes the difference, for if they allowed the kingdom of Satan to command their allegiance, there would be no possibility of conversion; if they surrendered themselves to Christ, however, they would have to take the first step in personal conversion. He called them to adopt a discipline based on the rule of Catholic faith and the pursuit of a holy life where sin is overcome, virtue acquired, and a strong character developed, with the grace of God. Their motto became "*Ad Majorem Dei Gloriam* — All for the Greater Glory of God."

Their commitment to Christ was enriched by meditating on the events of Christ's life described in the Gospels, especially on the saving Passion, death, and resurrection of Jesus. Ignatius insisted on a vigorous identification with the scenes in the Gospel — the different characters, how they looked, what they said, how they interacted with Christ, what the event looked like, what feelings were generated. This was more than simply imagining the occasion; it was an act of faith involvement in a revelation by Christ in a given situation.

Intensive and prayerful reading of the Gospels would open them to the many ways in which Jesus revealed himself. In our own time, Pope John Paul II caught the Ignatian insight in these words:

> The whole of Christ's life was a continual teaching: his silences, his miracles, his gestures, his prayer, his love for people, his special affection for the little and the poor, his acceptance of the total sacrifice on the Cross for the redemption of

the world, and his Resurrection are the actualization of his
word and the fulfillment of Revelation.

— *On Catechesis*, 9

These meditations were meant to help the exerciser realize that salvation is a gift of love that one should be willing to accept.

The final phase of the Exercises would lead the person to contemplate the mystery of Easter and its effect on his continuing life as a Jesuit. As the late Fr. Walter Burghardt, S.J., wrote:

The Exercises are not primarily an intellectual enterprise.
From beginning to end they are an experience. Ignatius asks
me to walk with the Jesus of Nazareth, talk with the Jesus of
Jerusalem, suffer with Jesus on the Cross, and rise with Jesus
from death. In his final meditation, Ignatius wants me to see
Jesus working within me "as a laborer," literally a collabora-
tor. As with the Fathers of the Church, my theology and my
spirituality must converge.

Through the Exercises, Ignatius prompted his followers to remove themselves from the distractions of the city and acquire an inner awareness of God's presence. He explained that they would have positive reactions of spiritual joy, and such consoling feelings would attach them to Christ. At the same time, they would also experience negative feelings of sadness and emptiness; these would lead them to a maturity where they stopped seeking the consolations of God, and instead would look for the God of consolations.

If they arrived at conversion and commitment, the seekers would then begin to appreciate God's will for them. This would happen through uniting their thinking and faith yearning with a quiet inner attention to signals that come from "resting in the Lord." Thus, knowing and doing God's will would be neither a mechanical, non-thinking "yes" to God nor an act of logic that required no prayerful listening to the impulse of the Holy Spirit.

The fundamental conversion that would ideally result from the first round with the Exercises was designed to be followed by a lifelong series of mini-conversions in which one would return to the Exercises for another prayerful step forward in one's spiritual growth. This would be brought about by the graces of the Holy Spirit and a deeper faith capacity to welcome God's loving transformation.

ADAPTING THE EXERCISES FOR TODAY

A contemporary Jesuit, Fr. Mark Link, has written an excellent little book, *Challenge: A Daily Meditation Based on the Spiritual Exercises of St. Ignatius* (Thomas More Publishing, Allen, TX). Fr. Link tells us that the Exercises were notes written by Ignatius for the directors of the thirty-day retreat in which the participants were led through the various steps of the Exercises. However, Ignatius also developed a year-long version for those unable to make the thirty-day retreat. Link's book is an adaptation of this approach for today's busy people.

He begins by noting the levels of awareness we all have. The first level is that of the senses: sight, taste, smell, touch, hearing. These are the five roads to knowledge. St. Thomas Aquinas wrote that there is nothing in the mind that is not first in the senses. The second level is the mind, where our thinking takes place. Here is the world of ideas and the activity of applying thoughts to everyday life. The third level is the heart — similar, but not identical, to what today is known as the subconscious. Related to this, the philosopher Blaise Pascal coined the famous statement, "The heart has reasons of which the mind does not know." The fourth level is the soul, the sanctuary of each person, where a deep encounter with the Holy Spirit can take place. The soul can be a temple of the presence of God and a setting where Christ's kingdom may be established.

The Senses

Sense, mind, heart, and soul participate in the adventure of prayer. The process of prayer could develop in many ways. One possibility is beginning with spiritual reading, such as Scripture or the life of a saint. Here, using the senses, one can enter into the world of Christ, picturing a scene from the Gospels: seeing Nazareth; entering with Jesus into the synagogue; being with the faith community; watching Mary observing her Son; joining in the singing of Psalms; hearing Jesus read from Isaiah's words that "the Spirit of the Lord is upon me" and closing the scroll, looking at everyone and saying that these words are fulfilled at that very moment. So the prayer begins by looking at Jesus, who is the face of God for us. We can comfortably converse with Christ. We can ask Mary to hold our hand and bring us to Christ. It might help some people to get a DVD of Franco Zeffirelli's glorious six-hour film, *Jesus of Nazareth*. There are over sixty scenes that can stimulate your faith and imagination. At the sense level, we make the Word of God real for ourselves — where we see Jesus, hear him, and find ourselves easing into a relationship with him.

The Mind

The use of the mind in prayer is applying what we experience in the first form of prayer. Many are already familiar with this way of praying. For example, we hear Jesus give us the eight ways to be happy: to be poor in spirit, meek, humble of heart, merciful, a peacemaker, a mourner, accepting of persecution, clean of heart. At first glance, our logic tells us this is no way to be happy. But as we watch Jesus — the face of God — practice all these virtues, we begin to think of how this fits in with our own behavior. Not only is this is a method of linking biblical rules of faith to Christian life; it also satisfies our need for meaning, since faith is a sunlight for reason. Again, recall St. Anselm's advice, "Believe, that you may understand."

The Heart

Our journey through sense and mind leads us next to our heart. This is the setting for speaking to God, not so much with words but with longings and yearnings for the Lord. This is what Cardinal Newman meant when he said prayer is "heart speaking to heart" (in Latin, *cor ad cor loquitur*). In this phase of prayer, we sense the life and movement of our hearts, much the same as a lover longs for the beloved. Perhaps an excellent example is Psalm 42, where the poet living in exile longs for God in his loneliness for the sights and sounds of the Temple feasts. He sees himself again in a grand procession, "with glad shouts and songs of thanksgiving, a multitude keeping festival" (v. 4). Like a thirsty deer searching for fresh water, the poet thirsts for the living God. This is heart language in prayer. The beauty of this phase of prayer is the feeling of being a free spirit. It's not as laborious as the beginning steps; we feel at ease with God and know we are being loved by the infinite freedom of God. Like an image drawn from Niagara Falls, that poet thrills with the majesty of heart prayer, "Deep calls to deep at the *thunder* of your cataracts" (v. 7).

The Soul

The fourth step of this form of prayer takes place in the soul, what T.S. Eliot calls the "stillpoint of the turning world." This is the zone of silence, where the quiet can be heard. It is the site of God as our anchor, our stronghold, our rock who speaks in silence. The noise of words is not needed; we are transported to a different level of discourse, like a contented older couple sitting on a swing and gazing at the August moon on a balmy summer evening. They have reached a communion of love beyond words, a transcendence that leaves all forms of insistence aside, a mellow union of pure joy.

The conversation with God in the soul is creative. God is essentially telling us, "Let it be... Let there be being." If we are moved to actually say something, we may borrow Mary's cry of joy, "*Magnificat!*"— "My soul magnifies the Lord." The simplicity of praise replaces the prior agonizing of what to say, see, do. The creative silence of God's Word is sufficient. During the time of the soul's prayer, we learn to be patient. We acquire the habit of taking time with God, of hearing deeply.

All these levels are true forms of prayer. The sequence is not absolute, for the complexity of human awareness and the infinite variety of God's way of reaching us forestalls rigidity and leaves us with God-given freedom to have a relationship with him that benefits our capacity. Fr. Link's daily meditations are guides to prayer that touch on the senses, mind, heart, and soul. Daily prayer with such guidance produces a habit of the heart in which the Holy Spirit works with us interiorly to become what God intended us to be, someone who lives by the rule of faith and yearns for a life of holiness in God.

Final Thoughts

In the last sixteen years of his life, Ignatius presided over an order that saw an astonishing growth in membership and influence. By the time of his death, a thousand Jesuits ministered in a number of colleges, as well as becoming missionaries to China, Japan, India, and major parts of North and South America. The stirring film *The Mission* dramatizes the political challenge they faced in Latin America. They mingled actively in the affairs of the world, following the maxim of St. Ignatius that more prudence and less piety were better than more piety and less prudence. Ignatius sternly stressed discipline, but never to the point of breaking a man's spirit or destroying his initiative. As a former soldier, he knew that the willingness to obey is the first step in learning to command, and his insight proved correct — for the Jesuits became a group of enterprising men who embraced leadership.

Ignatius judged people shrewdly and became one of the most influential men of modern history. The rugged, romantic soldier of Pamplona became a God-intoxicated religious leader. Few men have made such a transition so well. Few have ever done so much, as Ignatius said on his own behalf, "For the greater honor and glory of God."

PRAYER FOR GENEROSITY

By St. Ignatius of Loyola

Teach us, good Lord, to serve you as you deserve;
To give and not count the cost;
To fight and not heed the wounds;
To toil and not seek for rest;
To labor and not ask for any reward
Save that of knowing that we do your will.

FOR REFLECTION

1. How would apply the different phases of prayer (senses, mind, heart, soul) to your own way of praying?
2. What occurs to you when presented with developing a scene from the Gospels as a form of praying?
3. What draws you to listening to God in your prayer life?

For Contemplation

Anima Christi

Soul of my Savior, sanctify my breast.
Body of Christ, be thou my saving guest.
Blood of my Savior, bathe me in thy tide;
Wash me, ye waters flowing from his side.

Strength and protection may thy passion be;
O blessed Jesus, hear and answer me;
Deep in thy wounds, Lord, hide and shelter me
So might I never, never part from thee.

— Attributed to Bl. Bernadine of Feltran

Eight

THE EARTHY MYSTIC

St. Teresa of Ávila
(1515-1582)

A prioress may be very holy, yet incapable of governing a community. . . . In that case she should simply be removed from office.

— ST. TERESA, ADVICE TO VISITATORS

When Teresa entered the Convent of the Incarnation in Ávila, she found a congenial and easygoing community of women, good-spirited but not consumed with the spiritual fervor one might expect in a cloister. If anything, the convent was like a genteel hotel for the unmarried, upper-class women of Ávila. They did not observe the rules for cloister. They entertained guests in their rooms, treated the visiting area as though it were a hotel lobby, and some of them were given to wearing rings, bracelets, and necklaces. They thought nothing of leaving the convent to spend weekends and vacations with friends and relatives. The sisters recited only the required prayers and otherwise spent their time in visiting and keeping up on the news.

Being very personable and an extrovert, Teresa fell right in with the cheerful and casual ways of the community. She liked to laugh, sing, dance, and talk, so her gregarious spirit found a circle of like-minded women in the convent. She differed from them mainly in her mounting suspicion that this was not what convent living was all about.

After several years, her health began to fail. She wrote, "The change in the habits of my life and in my food proved harmful to my health. I began to have frequent fainting spells, and my heart was so seriously affected that everyone around me grew alarmed." Doctors seemed unable to help her, so she was taken to a famous woman healer in Becedas, whose use of violent purgatives nearly killed Teresa.

Subsequently afflicted by paralysis of her legs and a damaged constitution, Teresa returned to the convent, where she remained in that state for nearly three more years. She refused any further medical treatment, adopted a positive attitude toward her health, and prayed for a cure; slowly, her health returned and the paralysis disappeared.

While it is true that Teresa enjoyed the relaxed ways of the nuns, she always felt an attraction to meditative prayer and penance and was faithful to these practices with regularity. Imaginative or intellectual forms of meditation frustrated her; she was directed to practice imagining a scene from the life of Christ or think about a concept of Christian doctrine and relate it to her life and behavior.

Teresa dutifully practiced each of these forms of prayer for many years, but still intuitively felt she needed something deeper and could not find a spiritual director who understood her needs and could guide her forward. After twenty years of struggling with this meditation dilemma, she discovered the solution herself at last. One day, when meditating in the chapel, she noticed that a small painting of Christ being scourged at the pillar had been newly placed there. The image stirred her deeply with compassionate empathy for Jesus and she found herself moved into a profound tranquility, a non-conceptual, non-imaginative state of consciousness. She had stumbled onto what she was to write about as "The Prayer of Quiet."

Ironically, only after this personal discovery did she begin to meet spiritual directors, such as Francis Borgia and Peter Alcantara, who knew what she was talking about and could have pointed her in this direction in the first place. Perhaps it was just as well that she learned it on her own; that may have accounted for her ability to write a vivid description of the multiple processes of prayer, from initial meditations to what she called the "mystical marriage," a comparatively fixed state of conscious union with God.

Over the next decade, Teresa began to soar inwardly in her experience of God. Her meditations were sometimes accompanied by raptures, ecstasies, and trances. She was advised to write

---

STAY NEAR THE SACRED
HUMANITY OF CHRIST

God [the Father] desires that these graces must come to us from the hands of Christ, through his most sacred humanity, in which God takes delight.

Many times I have perceived this through experience. . . . A person should desire no other path, even if he is at the summit of contemplation; on this road he walks safely. All blessings come to us through our Lord. He will teach us, for in beholding his life we find that he is the best example.

[. . .] Let us consider the glorious St. Paul: it seems that no other name fell from his lips than that of Jesus, because the name of Jesus was fixed and embedded in his heart. Once I had come to understand this truth, I carefully considered the lives of some of the saints, the great contemplatives, and found that they took no other path.

Whenever we think of Christ we should recall the love that led him to bestow on us so many graces and favors, and also the great love God showed in giving us in Christ a pledge of his love; for love calls for love in return. Let us strive to keep this always before our eyes and to rouse ourselves to love him. For if at some time the Lord should grant us the grace of impressing his love on our hearts, all will become easy for us and we shall accomplish great things quickly and without effort.

— St. Teresa of Ávila, *LH* Vol. IV, pp.1483-84

---

both an autobiography and an account of her spiritual experiences. These books, especially *Interior Castle,* have become spiritual classics.

Teresa's Water Images of Prayer

Water Your Garden

One of Teresa's gifts was the capacity to reflect on her experiences of prayer, write about the steps she went through, and pass them on to her sisters — and, eventually, to the rest of the world in the books already mentioned, as well as *The Way of Perfection.* She liked to use everyday imagery that would help others to grow in prayer. Many find her metaphor of watering a garden to be helpful.

She wrote of four ways to do this: by taking water from a well; by obtaining water from an aqueduct; by drawing water from a stream near the garden; and finally, by receiving a gentle rain from heaven above. Each of these sources of water stand for a step in the progress of prayer.

The Well

Following her model, we see the effort to take a bucket, go to a well, and draw water. This is the active side of our beginning to pray (though at all times we are called and prompted to pray by the Holy Spirit). Jesus began the conversion to faith and prayer of the Samaritan woman at a well. As he led her to receive his revelation of himself as her friend and savior, he used the imagery of water that is like a fountain of grace rising up within her soul and leading her to burst forth with a prayer, "Sir, give me this water." (Jn 4:15) This invitation to grace was already on the lips of Isaiah when he urged his listeners, "Ho, every one who thirsts, come to the waters. . . . Seek the LORD while he may be found, call upon him while he is near" (Is 55:1, 6).

Just as Christian life begins by being baptized with water and the Spirit, so prayer originates in a recognition of our thirst for God. It is not just a pious act for Mother Teresa to require that the words *"I thirst"* appear beneath the Cross in all her chapels. It has a double meaning — reminding the worshipers that Jesus thirsts for our union with him, and we thirst for the living God. The first stages of prayer are marked by our actions, then, as we become aware of our dry souls, in need of the living waters of Christ to "moisturize" them.

The Aqueduct

Teresa then calls for obtaining water from an aqueduct that brings water from the mountains, surging into our lives. There is comfort, security, and confidence in knowing that the flow of fresh water from faraway heights comes to us in an unending flow. This period of prayer is like first love in which we experience the consolations of God's presence. We find it comparatively easy to rest in Christ. We are like the two disciples who are warmed by the presence of Christ. "Did not our hearts burn within us while he talked to us on the road, while he opened to us the Scriptures?" (Lk 24:32).

In this state of prayer, we are nourished with divine joy that seems to come to us in an endless flow from the mountain of God. We realize that we are not producing this joy; it is a gift from Christ, who wants to draw us permanently to himself. In those effortless times, prayer seems easy, and we beg Jesus to remain with us always. Like the Emmaus disciples, we pray, "Stay with us, for it is toward evening and the day is now far spent" (Lk 24:29). This religious experience is part of the adventure of prayer. Feeling God's presence attracts us to him and is a normal aspect of all who seek friendship with our Lord.

But dryness will come. Christ's call to discipleship involves denial of self, the carrying of our cross, and the challenge to follow him. We learn to find our joy in the demands of the eight beatitudes, as mentioned earlier: being poor in spirit, mourning life's losses, embracing humility, forgiving others seventy times seven, choosing purity of heart, finding all kinds of ways to make peace, and accepting persecution for the sake of Christ. The world finds these attitudes the least imaginable way to be happy, yet the saints show us there is no other path. Every beatitude is a path to prayer.

The Stream of Water

In the first three images, water comes to us from the well, the mountains, and now, a flowing stream. In this third picture, we benefit from the stream with little effort; we are allowed to be at rest in God alone, who becomes the active presence in our life of prayer. At the same time, our energies on behalf of the kingdom can be prodigious. The stories of many active saints witness this truth. The holy idleness of Mary is matched by the startling productivity of Martha in the same person. St. Paul was enraptured into the third heaven, while at the same time roaming the frontiers of the empire and establishing mission stations — some of which endure to this day as Christian centers, such as Thessalonica, Athens, and Rome. St. Frances Cabrini brought Christ to the great American cities and left behind 67 foundations and 1,500 Missionary Sisters of the Sacred Heart. Such men and women, resting in God by his endless stream of graces in their prayer lives, were also creative and evangelizing activists, spreading the Gospel and planting lasting foundations around the world.

At the same time, we need to note members of contemplative communities, whose prayerful influence flows from their cloisters to neighboring churches, and, in fact, to the whole world. This is most evident in the life of St. Thérèse of Lisieux, whose impact on the Church has been astounding, even though she lived in a cloister and died at twenty-four. Indeed, more things are wrought by prayer than this world dreams of.

The Gentle Rain

Teresa's fourth image, the gentle rain, describes those who are blessed with an enduring union with God. This stage is usually applied to those whom we call mystics. Certain people led by God into this privileged realm of friendship and union may at times become so absorbed in the divine presence that they feel drawn out of themselves into what we popularly call an ecstasy. St. Paul records his ecstatic experience for us:

> *I know a man in Christ who fourteen years ago was caught up to the third heaven — whether in the body or out of the body I do not know, God knows. And I know that this man was caught up into Paradise . . . and he heard things that cannot be told, which man may not utter.*
>
> — 2 COR 12:2-4

After Paul enjoyed this ecstasy in the Arabian wilderness, he was rudely jolted by the appearance of a mysterious "thorn in the flesh." He wrote that this thorn was meant to keep him from being too proud of the gifts he received. Many have speculated on the nature or identity of the thorn, but we will never know for sure what it was. What is clear is that it was severe enough to bother Paul fourteen years later — and keep him humble.

Teresa of Ávila also received a gift of ecstasy that she described as follows:

> *It pleased our Lord that I should see the following vision a number of times. I saw an angel near me on the left side, in bodily form. This I am not accustomed to see except very rarely. . . . In this vision it pleased the Lord that I should see*

it in this way. He was not tall, but short, marvelously beauti-
ful, with a face that shone as though he were one of the highest
angels, who seemed to be all on fire.... I saw in his hands a
long golden spear, and at the point of the iron, there seemed
to be a little fire. This I thought that he thrust into my heart
several times, and that it penetrated my entrails. When he
drew out the spear he left me on fire with a wondrous love
for God. The pain was so great that it caused me to utter sev-
eral moans; and yet so exceeding sweet that it is impossible to
desire to be rid of it, or my soul to be content with less than
God.

— E. Allison Peers,
Studies of the Spanish Mystics (London, 1927)

In the seventeenth century, Bernini, an outstanding sculp-
tor and architect, created the "St. Teresa in Ecstasy" altarpiece
in the Cornaro Chapel in the church of Santa Maria della Vit-
toria in Rome. He portrayed Teresa clothed from head to foot in
a hooded garment and swooning in ecstasy. Her feet are bare,
with the left one prominently shown. Her eyes are shut and
her mouth is open as she is absorbed by divine love. A winged
youth stands before her. In his right hand he holds an arrow,
symbolic of Jesus' love, pointed at her heart.

The impact of the sculpture needs to be seen in the back-
drop of the Counter-Reformation. After the tumult set off by
Martin Luther, the Church needed to recover from the Prot-
estant assault and resume her service to the cause of Christ.
The Council of Trent slowly created the building blocks of the
renewal of the Church. The bishops responded to the various
theological challenges, especially reaffirming the validity of
the priesthood, strengthening the theology of the Eucharist as
a sacrifice, and emphasizing the role of good works as well as
faith in the understanding of salvation. They also called for the

institution of seminaries, so that priests would be adequately prepared for their ministry. Pope St. Pius V published the *Roman Catechism* and the *Roman Missal* and oversaw the development of the Tridentine Mass. All these initiatives brought order and balance to the disarray caused by the Reformation.

Other movements, inspired by the Holy Spirit, augmented the bishops' daunting task. Ignatius founded the Jesuits, as we noted in the previous chapter. Missionaries fanned out over the world, spreading the Catholic faith to North and South America and parts of Asia and Africa. The new enthusiasm inspired the arts: Mozart, Palestrina, and others composed unforgettable church music, and, in a special way, Baroque sculpture and architecture infused the Catholic soul with hope and confidence.

Baroque church buildings and interior sculptures invited the congregations to viewer participation, dramatic lighting, and a display of emotions. More than anything else, these works of art and architecture were living sermons that conveyed Catholic doctrine in a winning manner. Now, a Catholic in Salzburg Cathedral could sit at Mass and hear the heart-melting harmonies of Mozart's *Mass in C* or Vivaldi's triumphant *Gloria* while surrounded by an army of saints and angels on pedestals and in niches almost flying into the air. What did all this say to a once-battered Church membership? In Latin, "*Confidite! Vici Mundum* — Be confident! I have overcome the world."

Who else could better summarize the Church's newfound confidence than the irrepressible Teresa of Ávila? How best could she be remembered than in the Bernini altarpiece that so energetically translated her inner spiritual marriage to God? Perhaps a comparative few in any generation could be lifted up to such spiritual heights, but in the wake of the many blows from outside and inside, the Teresian ecstasy raised up the heart of the entire Church.

Teresa's Second Career

As her spiritual life blossomed, so did her external mission as well. At the age of forty-eight, she began a second career as the founder of the reformed order of Carmelites, the discalced nuns who wore peasant-roped sandals instead of shoes. She found four women willing to join her in the first convent. She begged money from family and friends for a simple house to suit their needs, obtained the Pope's permission, and on August 24, 1562, moved with her novices into the new Carmel of St. Joseph.

Her Rule was cheerful, loving, and firm. The nuns slept on straw, ate no meat, and stayed in the convent. The tiled floor served as beds, tables, and chairs. She forbade begging but did install a revolving disk in the wall, upon which people could leave food if they wished. The sisters eked out a small living by spinning and needlework, putting their products on the disk for the taking, leaving the buyers to put whatever they wished in return. Even though austere, this cloister began attracting new members; the Carmelite provincial was so impressed with St. Joseph's that he asked Teresa to start another Carmel in Medina Del Campo.

While working on the details of the new Medina Carmel, Teresa was approached by the prior of the male Carmelite monastery, who was interested in ideas for reforming his own lax friars. He was accompanied by a second Carmelite, short, frail, and young, prompting Teresa to remark afterward, "Bless the Lord, for I have a friar and a half for my new monastery." The little man turned out to be John Alvarez — destined to become the famed St. John of the Cross, the crown and glory of the Discalced Carmelite Friars.

Over the next eighteen years, Teresa established sixteen more convents, amid a series of frustrations and anxieties that would have driven a lesser woman quite mad — or at least close to despair. Some of her difficulties came from the zoning boards of city councils, who feared that her convents, not having the normal sources of funding, would become local welfare cases.

The strongest opposition, however, came from the top administrators of the male Carmelites who followed the mitigated Rule. One report has it that they went so far as to smuggle in an agent who pretended to be seeking affiliation as a discalced nun, but who afterward testified that Teresa flogged her nuns and heard confessions as though she were a priest. Teresa was summoned before the Inquisition, only to hear, "You are acquitted of all charges. Go and continue your work." Hardly had she won that battle, though, than she was faced with the opposition of the papal nuncio. She wrote for protection to King Phillip II, who had read and loved her writings, was convinced of her saintliness, and granted her royal immunity. The papal nuncio changed his mind.

When not fighting political battles with these various opponents, Teresa was busy institutionalizing her eighteen convents and peppering them with her hard-won wisdom, collected now as Teresa's *Maxims*:

— *Never be obstinate, especially in unimportant matters.*
— *Be kind to others, but severe on yourself.*
— *Habitually make many acts of love, for they set the soul on fire and make it gentle.*

Perhaps the best insight into Teresa's practical nature can be found in the many volumes of her published letters. There, one finds the Teresa who argues with zoning boards, settles wills, negotiates purchases, and offers down-home advice — as in the case of a Cistercian nun who was collapsing into lengthy trances for no apparent reason. As one given to trances herself, Teresa looked into the matter and found out the woman was suffering from malnutrition due to ill-advised fasting. "Feed

St. Teresa of Ávila

the lady and she'll get better," said Teresa. And she did, never again to have a trance.

Teresa died at age sixty-eight, worn out and happy, on October 4, 1582. The Spanish government proclaimed her patroness of Spain in 1617. The Church canonized her in 1622.

PRAYER

Let nothing disturb you,
Let nothing cause you fear.
All things pass.
God is unchanging.
Patience obtains all:
Whoever has God needs nothing else.
God alone suffices.
        — BOOKMARK FOUND IN ST. TERESA'S PRAYER BOOK

FOR REFLECTION

1. As you reread St. Teresa's four levels of prayer through the images of water, how might that help you to grow in prayer with the help of the Holy Spirit?

2. In what way does the Church today need the confidence that was so present in the Church of the Counter-Reformation, especially as pertains to the role of prayer?

3. What aspects of St. Teresa's life appeal to you, and for what reasons?

FOR CONTEMPLATION

All the angels pray. Every creature prays. Cattle and beasts pray and bend the knee. As they come from their barns and caves they look up to heaven and call out, lifting up their spirit in their own fashion. The birds too rise and lift up themselves up to heaven: they open their wings, instead of hands, in the form of a cross, and give voice to what seems to be a prayer.

What more need to be said on the duty of prayer? Even the Lord himself prayed.

— TERTULLIAN (160-225), *LH* VOL. II, P. 250

Nine

THE ROLE OF LOVE IN PRAYER
St. Francis de Sales
(1567-1622)

*Divine love not only commands us again and again to love
our neighbor, but itself produces the love as its own image and
likeness and shed it over our hearts.*
— St. Francis de Sales,
Treatise on the Love of God

In the narrow streets of Padua's university district, a small
group of students prepared to ambush and haze a young man
whose quiet, studious ways at the law school aroused their envy
and distaste. It was the perfect setup for bullies and their hap-
less victim. However, this young man proved to be a superior
foil — if one may use a pun — in that he turned out to be a
superb swordsman who put them on the defensive and chased
them away, probably with a good laugh.

Clearly, they had been unaware that Francis de Sales was
a trained fencer. They probably would have been surprised to
know that he was also an expert horseman and smooth on the
dance floor.

The oldest of thirteen children, Francis as the firstborn son
occupied a privileged place in the household. His father wanted
Francis to replace him as a senator in the government of Savoy,
and toward that end, made sure that he had the requisite classics training and a degree in law. But by the time Francis had
come to Padua, he had resolved to be a celibate and planned to
be a priest; his dating skills and martial talents were put aside
in view of his new goals.

While depressed by his son's decision, the father was consoled that at least — thanks to some strings having been pulled by an influential cousin — Francis would be named to the prestigious post of Dean of St. Peter's Church in Geneva. Bishop Claude de Granier ordained Francis to the priesthood on December 18, 1593.

Those were the days when religion was a political football between Protestants and Catholics, and the Savoy region was a battleground for Calvinists and Catholics. The shifting tides of wars saw a game of musical chairs: if a Calvinist leader won, he attempted to force all citizens to follow his faith; likewise, a victorious Catholic would strive to bring the Calvinists back to Rome.

This was the seesaw religio-political world in which Francis de Sales pursued his priestly ministry. The axiom of the day was "*Cuius region, eius religio,*" which (paraphrased) means that the religion of the people should follow the religion of the king. The newly ordained Francis began his priestly career with the freshly victorious Catholic Duke of Savoy. Missionary priests were needed, especially the area of the south shore of Lake Geneva, populated mostly by convinced Calvinists. Political pressure would not be enough to force these people to become Catholics; the situation needed systematic, vigorous evangelization.

Francis followed the traditional tactic of moving from town to town, visiting Catholic families to encourage them, while using their homes as bases for outreach to Calvinists. But he soon found that process slow, inefficient, and frustrating. Not enough people were being touched on a regular and persuasive basis. Worrying through this problem, Francis discovered what Luther had already known and mastered: namely, the power of the print medium to spread ideas, change minds, and convert people.

Francis became a pamphleteer, taking advantage of a communications medium that had been around for over a century but had scarcely been used by the Church to implement its mission. He began writing what amounted to a weekly newsletter, containing a point of Catholic doctrine in simple and lucid prose, along with arguments against the opposition. For the first few months he experimented with the idea of having copies reproduced by hand. When he saw how successful the handwritten materials were, he then moved to print.

This was the beginning of his career as a religious journalist and the reason why he is today the patron saint of journalists. In realizing the power of the printed word, Francis evolved into a defender of the Catholic faith. Since he could never hope to be physically present to so many thousands of people on a regular and consistent basis, he did the next best thing. He came to them in pamphlets, books, and letters. This may seem self-evident to us, but at that time, it was a new idea. For now, the printing press was not just an instrument for reproducing the works of the past; it could serve to evangelize the newly literate populations of the middle-class urban centers.

In addition, Francis found within himself another unsuspected talent; he happened to be an unusually appealing public speaker. His training in classics supplied him with the abundant imagery of the poets, and his years in law school taught him the arts of persuasion. But he was unique in his decision to use a low-key, laid-back speaking style, in contrast to the over-dramatic, polemical approach that was the accepted preaching method of the day. Francis had the common touch and a sure sense of where his audience was, as well as a poet's gift for choosing down-home comparisons, as is evident in his oft-quoted advice about motivation — "A spoonful of honey works far better than a barrel of vinegar." Actually, his conversational speaking style was the kind looked for in today's ideal TV presenters: relaxed and natural, pungent without being pugnacious, a capacity to be critical of the opposition without being shrill or strident.

He delivered thousands of sermons in this manner in hundreds of cities and towns, knowing instinctively that when the audience has seen and heard the speaker, the follow-up pamphlets and books will make more sense. The calmness of his talks and the sweet reasonableness of his soft-sell presentation have led many commentators to speak mellifluously of the "gentle de Sales." But this is a misleading characterization, for it implied that Francis leaned to the sentimental; in reality, he was far more a contained volcano than a pitcher of syrup. His was a "gentleness" only by contrast with the angry polemics and theatrical posturing that prevailed around him. He was a brilliant, disciplined communicator whose writings remain as an admired example of French literature. As a speaker, he had a knack for helping people hear the truth and come to faith.

The Laity as Evangelizers

Francis believed passionately in the capacity of the laity to serve as evangelizers for the Faith. It was this conviction that moved him to write a masterpiece of spiritual growth in a language immediately available to the laity: *Introduction to the Devout Life*. Written in an uncomplicated prose, his book offers systematic and sensible advice on how to meditate, develop a Christian value-oriented character, and surrender oneself to the impulses of grace.

He possessed a genius for writing about mysticism without sounding mysterious, thereby making available for millions of laity spiritual insights once reserved to those in cloisters. So successful has been this work and his *Treatise on the Love of God* on the awareness of succeeding generations that they have become the core literature of "The Salesian School of Spirituality." His books and his virtuous life account for Rome's naming him a Doctor of the Church.

By creating a trained laity in the arts of spirituality and skills for evangelizing, Francis again multiplied his effectiveness, as he did in using the print medium. He had no messiah complex that would have vainly reserved everything to his

---

TRUE AND FALSE DEVOTION

I say that devotion must be practiced in different ways by the nobleman and by the working man, by the servant and by the prince, by the widow, by the unmarried girl and the married woman. But even this distinction is not sufficient; for the practice of devotion must be adapted to the strength, to the occupation and to the duties of each one in particular.

Tell me, please, my Philothea [God Lover], whether it is proper for a bishop to want to lead a solitary life like a Carthusian; or for married people to be no more concerned than a Capuchin about increasing their income; or for a working man to spend his whole day in church like a religious; or on the other hand for a religious to be constantly exposed like a bishop to all the events and circumstances that bear on the needs of our neighbor. Is not this sort of devotion ridiculous, unorganized and intolerable? Yet this absurd error occurs very frequently, but in no way does true devotion, my Philothea, destroy anything at all. On the contrary, it perfects and fulfills all things. In fact if it ever works against, or is inimical to, anyone's legitimate station and calling, then it is very definitely false devotion.

The bee collects honey from flowers in such a way as to do the least damage or destruction to them, and he leaves them whole, undamaged and fresh, just as he found them. True devotion does still better. Not only does it not injure any sort of calling or occupation, it even embellishes and enhances it.

— St. Francis de Sales,
Introduction to a Devout Life, LH Vol. III, p. 1318

St. Francis de Sales

personal presence. He relied on the power of God's presence through the printed word and the evangelizing potential of the thousands of people growing in holiness through his spiritual direction.

At the same time, Francis understood the value of being open and available to people. When he became the bishop of Geneva, he did not retreat into a hidden administrative mold. At home, he practiced an open-door policy. On pastoral mission, he was a thoroughgoing populist, reaching out eagerly to all people and relentlessly inviting them to come to him so he could take them to Christ and the Church. He said, "We bishops must be like those large public drinking fountains, where all have the right to come for water."

His thirty-one-year ministry as priest and bishop in the Lake Geneva area proved to be successful. With a slight but forgivable exaggeration he said, "When we arrived there were no more that fifteen Catholics in the Chablis area; now, there are not more than fifteen Calvinists." He was substantially right. Left unsaid is the fact that the religious stabilization of the territory ended, for the time being, the cycle of religious wars.

THE CALL TO HOLINESS

It is therefore quite clear that all Christians in any state or walk of life are called to the fullness of Christian life and to the perfection of love, and by this holiness a more human manner of life is fostered also in earthly society. In order to reach this perfection the faithful should use the strength dealt out to them by Christ's gift, so that following in his footsteps and conformed to his image, doing the will of God in everything, they may wholeheartedly devote themselves to the glory of God and to the service of their neighbor. Thus the holiness of the People of God will grow in fruitful abundance.

— *THE CHURCH*, 40

This quote from the Second Vatican Council supports the vocation of all the members of the Church to a life of holiness, sustained by prayer and loving service to others. This was a dream that motivated Francis de Sales in his lifetime. He believed that all Catholics could be holy, not just those in convents and monasteries. The ideal of holiness for all is stated by Christ himself.

> *"Be perfect, just as your heavenly Father is perfect."*
> — MT 5:48

> *"Be merciful as your heavenly Father is merciful."*
> — LK 6:36

God the Father made the call to holiness for everyone eminently clear, and St. Peter echoed this invitation. Their words are addressed to every one of God's people.

> *"As he who called you is holy, be holy yourselves in every aspect of your conduct, for it is written, 'Be holy because I am holy.'"*
> — 1 PET 1:15-16; LEV 11:45

In calling people to holiness, Francis de Sales emphasized the role of love in prayer. He instinctively created simple pictures to illustrate great truths, comparing the love of God to romantic love:

> *The thoughts of those moved by natural human love are almost completely fastened on the beloved. Their hearts are filled with passion for the loved one, their mouths full of praises. When the beloved is gone they express their feelings in love letters, and can't pass a tree without carving the name of their beloved in its bark. Thus, also, those who love God can never stop thinking about him, aspiring to him, and speaking*

about him. If they could they would engrave the name of Jesus
on the hearts of all humankind.

*The key to loving God is prayer. By turning your eyes to
God in meditation, your whole soul will be filled with God.
Begin all your prayers in the presence of God. Retire from
your busy life into the solitude of your own heart, even while
outwardly engaged in discussions with others and secretly
whisper to God. Prayer and deeds go together. To be an angel
in prayer and a beast to people is to go lame on both legs....*

The last advice Francis gave on his death bed was:
"Humility."

> — ADAPTED FROM *CATHOLIC ONLINE*'S REFLECTION ON
> THE SAINT'S FEAST, JANUARY 24

In 1604, while preaching a Lenten retreat in Dijon, Francis met the recently widowed Jane de Chantal. He became her
spiritual adviser and with her became a co-founder of the nuns'
Order of the Visitation. In 1622 Francis agreed to make a physically demanding journey with the Duke of Savoy to meet the
French king for the purpose of gaining some concessions. The
exertions took their toll, though, and Francis was forced to stop
at the Visitation convent in Lyons, where he died. Pope Alex-
ander VII canonized him on April 19, 1665, and Pope Pius IX
declared him a Doctor of the Church in 1877.

For a modern Church finding itself in the midst of a communications revolution, Francis de Sales looms as a friendly and
encouraging figure. He was wise enough to take advantage of
the relatively new print medium to serve evangelization. Above
all, he proved to be a man of prayer in the midst of a very busy
life that involved lots of travel and continuously adapting his
approach amid a succession of new experiences. Nonetheless,
he filled the demands of his office — dealing with all kinds of
people, writing books and pamphlets, and preaching thousands

of sermons with the ideal of praying always. He made his work a prayer, but he also filled the spaces and pauses of busyness with quick "darts" of prayer, like the old desert monks advised. He set aside quiet times for solitary, silent adoration of God and made prayer a habit of his heart. All his waking moments were a consecration of himself to God. He mastered the concentration needed to be present to his work and to his Lord at the same time.

He never vainly attributed such achievements to himself. He knew the gifts all came in from a divine stream, governed by the strong, yet gentle impulses of the Holy Spirit. He preached what he practiced and was a gentleman to his audience — conscious of each person's unique needs, giving them, one by one, that courtly courtesy that honored differences and yet fed their universal spiritual hunger for God. He understood perfectly that we must begin with humility so we can end with love.

PRAYER

Father,
You gave Francis de Sales the spirit of compassion
to befriend all men and women on the way to salvation.
By his example, lead us to show your gentle love
in the service of others. Amen.

FOR REFLECTION

1. What has been your experience in trying to pray always, especially in those times when your life is burdened with distractions?

2. When did you discover that the love of God is essential to the conversations with the Lord in your prayer? What circumstances brought this about?

3. What paths have you pursued to acquire the virtue of humility? What taught you to distinguish between true and false humility?

For Contemplation

Let us be what we are and let us be it well, to do honor to the Master whose work we are.

Try to convince yourself… that God wants you to serve him just as you are, both by practices that are suited to your state in life, and by the actions that go with it. Once you are convinced of this, you must bring yourself to a tender affection for your state in life and for everything about it, out of love for him that wills it so.

— St. Francis de Sales, as cited online by Margaret S. Margeton in her article, "St. Francis de Sales and the Universal Call to Holiness" (*Catholic Faith*, March/April 1999).

Ten

SMALL DEEDS — GREAT LOVE
St. Thérèse of Lisieux
(1873-1897)

*After my death I shall let fall a shower of roses. . . . I shall
come back to earth and teach others how to love Love.*
— ST. THÉRÈSE OF LISIEUX, *THE STORY OF A SOUL*

What do you say about a twenty-four-year-old nun who died of tuberculosis? As one of her Carmelite sisters who paused outside her sickroom wondered, "Thérèse will die soon. What will the Prioress be able to write for her obituary? She entered our convent, lived here, and died. There really is no more to say."

Yet within a few months of her death, so great a storm of interest and affection for Thérèse began that a Vatican cardinal declared, "We must hasten to canonize Thérèse, otherwise we shall be anticipated by the voice of the people." The Vatican, indeed, broke its traditional rule of not starting a canonization process until fifty years after a person's death, by naming Thérèse a saint in 1925. (Had Thérèse been alive, she would have been only 52.)

Her obituary had a lot to do with this, because it was more than a death notice. It happened to be a journal in which Thérèse had recorded some childhood memories, girlhood experiences, and a series of practical lessons about convent living. This journal, titled *The Story of a Soul*, had been written for her older sisters, also Carmelites, and sent out to other convents as a memorial book. But it soon had an extraordinary impact upon its readers, and demand for it was overwhelming. By 1932, over 800,000 copies of the book were in circulation, plus 2.5 million copies of an abridged version in the original language alone. At the time of her canonization, the book had been translated into thirty-five languages. These figures have enormously increased since then.

What accounted for this unforeseen interest in *The Story of a Soul*? Two things that the young nun promised, both of which she has fulfilled.

The first promise Thérèse made in her book is perhaps the best known — "After my death I shall let fall a shower of roses." People took her at her word and sought miracles and spiritual favors through her intercession. By 1925, the Carmel at Lisieux had some 3,000 pages of documented answers to such prayers: cures of cancer, ulcers, blindness, meningitis, and other ailments (with medical affidavits) — as well as religious conversions and just plain peace of heart. Stories came in of rescues, conversions, and cures . . . liberation from prisons, plagues, and floods . . . in Chinese villages, Moslem strongholds in Algeria, Indian cities, South African farms, and other sites from Manchuria, the Solomon Islands, and Thailand to Alaska and New York.

Another of Thérèse's promises no doubt contributed to further affection for her: "I shall come back to earth to teach others to love Love." Millions have felt that love and returned it to her enthusiastically — such as the Madagascar orphans and Japanese lepers who went without rice to make a donation to build her basilica in Lisieux; the African priests in the Congo who placed themselves under her protection; or the Canadian city that sent a thousand pilgrims to celebrate the anniversary of her canonization. Protestants were touched; the Anglicans at Walsingham reverently exhibited a piece of her blanket. And in Iran, a Shiite Moslem — whose faith is exceptionally hostile to making images — kept a picture of Thérèse publicly posted. Testifying that she had brought him a cure, he said, "Neither Mohammed nor the prophets outweigh this little saint."

This brings us to the third and, clearly, most important area of Thérèse's exceptional influence — her life.

The storyline is comparatively uneventful. Born in Alençon, France, the youngest of nine children, Thérèse Martin — daughter of Louis Martin, a watchmaker, and his wife, Zelie Guerin — was raised in Lisieux by her elder sisters and an aunt after the death of her mother when Thérèse was five. Outwardly, her childhood was marked by the usual comforts and annoyances of cozy, middle-class French family life in the nineteenth century.

Her father was a devout Catholic and encouraged a sense of piety in the family, with the result that the two eldest daughters entered the Carmel at Lisieux. Early on, Thérèse had a precocious interest in spiritual matters. It was also clear she possessed unusual powers of concentration, so that beneath the flowery femininity and language of endearment that was the fashion of the times, there resided inside her a granite-hard resolve and a single-minded determination to pursue an inward attraction to God. With the utmost candor, she could say, "I have never refused the good God anything" and mean it. Not that she was immune to moods and expected tantrums, as might be expected of a growing young girl; but after the storm, she resolutely returned to the grand passion of her life — union with Love.

At the age of fourteen, she began making noises about joining her sisters at the Lisieux Carmel, It did not seem to matter to her that she was too young, or that her doting father would miss her, or that prudence and common-sense experience would demand a delay. Moreover, some worried that having three nuns from the same family, in a small Carmel limited to twenty-one nuns, would be just a bit too much. Thérèse campaigned vigorously, however, to achieve her goal. First, she convinced her father. Then, she found an unexpected ally in the Prioress, Marie de Gonzague — who, unaccountably, decided to support Thérèse's wish. But Thérèse found strong opposition from the places one might reasonably expect it: from both her pastor and her bishop, who argued simply that she was too young.

Around this time her father took her and her older sister on a pilgrimage to Rome, a month-long trip that was largely a sight-seeing holiday for the prosperous Catholics on the tour. Marie de Gonzague advised Thérèse to ask the Pope himself for permission, and this she resolved to do. Her account of the trip revealed her singlemindedness, because she had relatively little to record about the glorious art and architecture that would normally have touched her otherwise impressionable sensitivities. Coming from a brother-less environment, Thérèse coped for the first time with the attention of young men, one of whom fell in love with her during their travels, as Celine testified at the canonization trial. Thérèse was moved but determined to be a Carmelite; she alluded to the incident thus: "I feel that my heart is easily caught by tenderness, and where others fail, I would fail too. . . . I am no stronger than the others."

In Rome, the pilgrims were presented to Pope Leo XIII. Each pilgrim came and knelt before the Pope while the Vicar General introduced the person. Then, the Pope would say a few words, bless the pilgrim, and bestow a medal. Just before Thérèse's turn, the Vicar General announced that no one should speak to the Pope — at the same instant Celine whispered to her sister, "Speak!"

So Thérèse did. "Holy Father, in honor of your jubilee, let me enter the Carmel at age fifteen —"

But the vicar interrupted her. "Your Holiness, the superiors at Carmel are addressing this question."

"Very well, " said Pope Leo, "let the superiors decide."

Thérèse, not to be deterred, clasped her hands on the Pope's knees and spoke to him as though he were her own father. "If you said yes, everyone would be willing."

Leo XIII just looked at her and finally said, "Well . . . well . . . You will enter if it is God's will."

As they led her away, the Pope laid his hands on Thérèse's lips, a gesture hard to interpret in retrospect. She was deeply disappointed and compared the ruins of Pompeii to her own mood — "I longed to walk among the ruins and ponder how transient all things are."

Once home, she waited out the weeks and months for a reply, anxiously checking the mail each day. The bishop's approval finally came on December 28, but she would have to wait to begin until after Lent. On April 9, 1888, Thérèse entered the Carmel. She later wrote, "My dream at last was realized, and peace flooded my soul . . . It has never left me these eight and a half years."

Finally, she had entered a solitude to which she was totally convinced God had called her. The enviable concentration with which she had been gifted now found a worthy object — or, better said, subject, for the God of love laid absolute claim to her affections, and she never wavered in her attention to his call. Her inward journey can scarcely be charted; it remains a mystery, like noticing the gleam of a candle in the noonday sun. At best, we can only intuit it and catch some light from her writings and the plain details of her life.

She made her novitiate, professed her vows, and formally "took the veil," at about the same time her father took ill and was placed in a sanitarium. Three years after her entry, a flu epidemic ravaged the convent, killing three of the nuns. Thérèse's own health broke down due to overstrain in caring for her sisters. Then, her father died, and her sister became Prioress, at which point Celine joined her three sisters in the Carmel. In June 1897, at the request of her sister Pauline, Thérèse began writing *The Story of a Soul* and completed it just before her death on September 30, 1897. On October 4, she was buried in the town cemetery in Lisieux.

Doctor Thérèse

On October 19, 1997, Pope John Paul II conferred on St. Thérèse of Lisieux the title of Doctor of the Church. The requirements for this title include being a person of outstanding holiness who shows depth of doctrinal content in writings and produces

"I WILL BE LOVE IN THE HEART OF THE CHURCH."

When I had looked upon the mystical body of the Church, I recognized myself in none of the members which Saint Paul described, and what is more, I desired to distinguish myself more favorably within the whole body. Love appeared to me to be the hinge for my vocation. Indeed I knew the Church had a body composed of various members, but in this body the necessary and more noble member was not lacking. I knew that the Church had a heart and that such a heart appeared to be aflame with love. I knew that one love drove the members of the Church to action, that if this love were extinguished, the apostles would have proclaimed the Gospel no longer, the martyrs would have shed their blood no more. I saw and realized that love sets off the bounds of all vocations, that love is everything, that this same love embraces every time and every place. In one word, that love is everlasting.

Then, nearly ecstatic with supreme joy in my soul, I proclaimed: O Jesus, my love, at last I have found my calling: my call is love. Certainly I have found my proper place in the Church, and you gave me that very place, my God. In the heart of the Church, my mother. I will be love, and thus I will be all things, as my desire finds its direction.

— St. Thérèse of Lisieux, *LH* Vol. IV, p. 1451

St. Thérèse of Lisieux

a substantial amount of writing both free from error and faithful to Tradition. Thérèse possessed all three attributes. Even among other saints, her holiness shone brightly. Her writings reflected the depth of God's merciful love perhaps better than anyone had done before. Finally, her writings proclaimed God's truths, often in an original manner.

Thérèse's early fame was associated with the thousands of answers to prayers received through her intercession. She indeed poured a "shower of roses," an abundance of replies to prayers of countless people. One author referred to this phenomenon as a "storm of glory." While that is still true of her, we have an even deeper appreciation of her life and value:

> *Far more than for the power of her intercession, she is known for the depth of her insight into the mystery of Who God Is. She knew God deeply because she loved him deeply. "How can I fear a God," she asked, "who is nothing but Mercy and Love?" That was her definition of God, "Mercy and Love." Everything else in her Little Way and in her spiritual doctrine follows from that profound intuition. She will be known as Doctor of God's Merciful Love.*
>
> — BISHOP PATRICK V. AHERN, *THÉRÈSE, DOCTOR OF THE CHURCH* (WWW.CATHOLIC.NET; 1997)

THÉRÈSE'S REMARKABLE VIEW OF HEAVEN

Thérèse did not accept the idea of heaven as a state of eternal rest:

> *How could I rest as long as there are souls to save? If heaven is rest I don't want to go there. I will spend my heaven doing good upon earth.*

She gives us a dynamic picture of the Communion of Saints. In heaven, we will participate in God's infinite holiness and mercy. We will remember our faults and sins that God has forgiven. This will make us sympathetic to those we have left behind and help us implore God to give this same tenderness to others that we have received. In a letter to her spiritual brother, Maurice, she wrote, "I will love you more once I am in heaven than I ever could on earth. The saints never stop protecting and praying for us."

These words of Thérèse should help all of us to regain a sense of the grand community of all those in heaven and earth who form with us a bond of grace that flows from God's throne of mercy and love. There is no impenetrable wall between heaven and earth. Our departed relatives and friends are far more able to love us from there than they could on earth. Nothing impedes their affection. They see us having the same struggles they had; only now, they can obtain help for us in our battles. God does not want his love bottled up in heaven. He cannot give us what we do not desire. Love never forces an entrance. Our heavenly friends side with us, praying for our needs, lending their desire for God to the weakness of our own yearnings.

Our prayer life needs to be open to Thérèse's remarkable vision of the proximity of heaven's world to our own — to the compassion of Mary, the angels, and the saints, who simply echo what the Holy Trinity wants us to have. The whole point of creation and redemption revolves around the merciful love of God. No one is more forgiving. No one can love us more. Heaven's music is an eternal concern for our happiness and fulfillment.

THE "LITTLE WAY" TO HOLINESS

Thérèse developed a simple plan for prayer and sanctifying each day. She called it her *Little Way* because it was for ordinary people and not meant to be an elitist method. Basically, it was a matter of small deeds and big love. Most everyday acts are down-to-earth forms of behavior. Even famous people known for magnificent achievements pass their days doing unremark-able things. The president still puts on his pants one leg at a time. The Oscar-winning actress generally uses a knife and fork like anyone else. They are just as pleased with a little fan letter as our relatives are when we remember their birthdays.

Thérèse provided a spiritual method as within the grasp of the working man and woman as it would be for an opera star or a bank president: turn each daily act into a prayer by doing it with deep love for God and for those we serve. As Blessed Teresa of Calcutta often said, "Do little things with great love." For every act of love, we receive from God a greater capacity to love and be loved. With each act of love we lay up treasures in heaven, because such acts bond us with God and guide us on the way to our true homeland, which is life with God in eter-nity. It is the easiest way to think of holiness, because we were born to love and be loved... so we are doing what comes (super) naturally.

Much is made of the term "little" in Thérèse's life — Lit-tle Thérèse, the "Little Way." Actually, this little woman was a giant. "Little" never meant diminutive or unimportant in her case. It really referred to simplicity, a trait found in geniuses, whether religious or otherwise. Her culture and religious tra-ditions were stuffed with "doodads" as suffocating as the Vic-torian drawing rooms of the day. Her "little," then, is more akin to the "small is beautiful" and "less is more" tastes of our own culture. This is one reason she has captivated intellectuals while retaining mass appeal at the same time. With unusual clarity, she made the depths of interior prayer and selfless love as available to the mighty as to the humble — and they both have loved her and the Christ to whom she points. What more could one expect of a saint?

PRAYER

Good saints, hear my prayer. You have already seen the glorious life that waits for me in heaven. I know you found it beyond anything you might have dreamed of here on earth. You made it. You succeeded. Please help me as I struggle in my journey. Pray for me to our merciful Father. I look forward to meeting all of you in heaven. Amen.

— Monica Dodds, *Praying In the Presence of Our Lord With St. Thérèse of Lisieux* (Our Sunday Visitor, 2004), p. 57

FOR REFLECTION

1. As you read again St. Thérèse's ideas of heaven, how do they compare with your own thoughts?
2. How might you incorporate her "Little Way" of prayer into your own life? What challenges would it make for you?
3. Even though she was a cloistered Carmelite in nineteenth-century France, what from her experiences do you find relevant to your own life?

FOR CONTEMPLATION

Certainly, Thérèse herself imitated Mary. A priest who knew her well called her "a ravishing miniature of the Virgin Mary." How she loved the Mother of Jesus! With a hand that trembled and could no longer dip her pen in the inkwell, she picked up her pencil for the last time, and this is what she wrote: "O Mary, if I were the Queen of Heaven and you were Thérèse, I would want to be Thérèse so that you might be the Queen of Heaven." Famous last written words, worthy of a Doctor of the Church, easy to understand and easy to remember — and such an astonishing thing to think of saying!

— Bishop Patrick V. Ahearn

Eleven

Praying With Mary
Mary's Song — The Magnificat

Almost all the words that Mary speaks in the Gospels are prayers. Among those prayers, her Magnificat is so prominent that the Church around the world sings it every evening at Vespers. Mary's Song occurs during her visit to her cousin Elizabeth, now miraculously pregnant in her old age with John the Baptist.

Trappist monk Thomas Merton composed a poem, *The Quickening of John the Baptist*, that retells the story of Mary's visit to Elizabeth. He pictures the newly pregnant Mary, hurrying to help Elizabeth with the birth of her child. Merton sees her leaving behind the lemon trees, the yellow fishing boats, the oil-presses, and the wine-smelling yards. He asks her what truth lies behind her eyes, gray as doves.

The moment Mary greeted Elizabeth, the child leaped in her cousin's womb. Merton likened Mary's salutation to a monastery bell, a call to a faith experience. The unborn John wakes in his mother's body and bounds with self-discovery. What was there about Mary's voice? What secret syllable awoke John's faith? What was it like to be washed in the Spirit of God while yet in the womb? How did he come to know the Jesus cloistered in Mary's womb?

Merton required no words from John. John's body talk — the ecstasy of that leap in the womb — said it all. He revealed the sheer joy of being filled with God's Spirit. Like him, before such a mystery, we live as listeners to heaven. We do not first understand this with our heads but with the faith in our hearts.

The Visitation

Mary, the God-bearer (*Theotokos*), brings her virgin presence and her child to wake us up and prompt us to a song of joy.

Elizabeth praises Mary: "Blessed is she who believed that there would be a fulfilment of what was spoken to her from the Lord" (Lk 1:45). Mary's faith made possible the entry of salvation into our world. Her *yes* to the angel came from the faith in her obedient heart. "Let it be done," she said. The "let it be done" is a creation expression. It echoes God's creative words in Genesis 1: "Let it be!" Let there be being. Mary's joy moves her to repeat that command, "Let there be the Son." With her *yes*, the Holy Spirit takes our human nature from her and weds it to the divine nature of the Son of God, whose divine Person unites the two natures into himself.

— ADAPTED FROM FR. McBRIDE'S COMMENTARY ON LUKE'S
GOSPEL, *THE HUMAN FACE OF JESUS*
(OUR SUNDAY VISITOR, 1992), PP. 20-22

Now, hearing Elizabeth's words of blessing, Mary broke into her unforgettable song and praised God with her *Magnificat*.

This is the song both of the Mother of God and of the Church; the song of the Daughter of Zion and the new People of God; the song of thanksgiving for the fullness of graces poured out in the economy [the plan] of salvation and the song of the "poor" whose hope is met by the fulfillment of the promises made to our ancestors and to his posterity forever.

— CCC 2619

MARY'S SONG (LK 1:46-55)

"My soul magnifies the Lord,
and my spirit rejoices in God my Savior . . ."

Mary's attention moves from herself to the God who has blessed her with an incredible gift. Her cry of joy is like the unrestrained roar of happiness at a victory score at a game, at the news a war is over, at the completion of vows taken at a wedding or an ordination. Many wonderful stories surround the birth of her Son. All of them express the humble gift of one's soul.

O.Henry tells the Christmas story of two lovers, one of whom sells her long hair to buy a watch for her beloved, even as he sacrifices all he has to buy a comb for her hair. The legendary Drummer Boy offers Jesus the best gift he knows — to play his drum, and thereby to glorify Christ. Our Lady's Juggler could think of nothing better than to go to the local monastery church and entertain the Virgin and Child with his juggling act. The monks pause from chanting the Psalms and look on, amazed, as the statues come alive and fill the shrine with warmth and joy.

Mary's Song found others hoping to magnify the Lord with their simple presents. The shepherds brought Jesus some sheep and lambs to warm the stable. Their greater gift was their humble faith and gratitude for the greatest gift in history. The angels did what they always do best — sing heavenly music. They wanted the world to know how God's Love had come to earth. The Magi brought Jesus royal gifts, but they really magnified the Lord with the energy and faith that brought them hundreds of miles to adore the baby.

And now for ourselves. We give each other presents at Christmas, and still we wonder how to be like Mary's Song. Magnify the Lord by giving Jesus something of yourself — like the shepherds, angels, Magi, the Little Drummer Boy, or O.Henry's generous lovers. Foolishly, we sometimes give others "a piece of our minds." Why not love away that crust over your hearts and give Jesus your whole self? Then, your soul will rejoice in God your Savior.

"... *for he has regarded the low estate of his handmaiden,*
For behold, henceforth all generations will call me blessed;
  for he who is mighty has done great things for me,
and holy is his name."

When the Holy Spirit touched the womb of Mary 2,000 years ago, a prediction arose from the lips of the Virgin: "All generations will call me blessed." In this, Our Blessed Mother was more right that she might have imagined. Mary of Nazareth, the mother of Jesus Christ, true God and true man, is the most celebrated and venerated woman in all of history. Today, attention to Mary is more pronounced than ever.

Every day, the faithful recite over two *billion* Hail Marys; millions go to Mary's shrines — annually, around five million pilgrims flock to Lourdes in France, and ten million show up at Guadalupe in Mexico City. Millions more travel to Fatima, Czestochowa, Medjugorje, and American sites such as Our Lady of the Snows in Belleville, IL, and the National Shrine of the Immaculate Conception in Washington, DC.

More girls are named for Mary than any other historical figure. New books about Mary appear regularly. Artists, composers, sculptors, poets, and architects have produced hymns, poems, paintings, statues, and cathedrals honoring Mary. Andea Bocelli's Christmas CD starts with four heart-melting versions of the *Ave Maria*. Many a Catholic wedding concludes at the shrine of Our Lady to pray for a happy marriage while a Marian hymn is sung. In recent times, Mary was chosen for Christmas cover stories by *TIME* and a special edition of *LIFE* magazines.

We call Mary blessed because God, who is mighty, has done great things for her. The closer we get to Mary, the nearer she brings us to Christ. God called her to give Jesus to the world. Mary does not draw attention to herself, but rather to her Son.

Those whose prayers are answered by Mary's intercession find themselves attracted to Jesus, especially in the Mass and adoration of the Blessed Sacrament.

This love for our Blessed Lord extends to the Church. If you want to be a good Catholic, stay near Mary. If you want motivation to go regularly to Confession and weekly Mass, turn to Mary. If you want to have a social conscience and do works of love, justice, and mercy, go to Mary. She will give you your marching orders. And you will give up profanity because she tells you, "Holy is his name."

> *"And his mercy is on those who fear him*
>   *from generation to generation.*
> *He has shown strength with his arm,*
> *he has scattered the proud in the imagination*
>   *of their hearts . . ."*

Mary connected God's gift of humility with the graces of being called "blessed." Her humility is even closer to her words about mercy and arrogance. She knew her Old Testament and the many stories of God's mercy to her ancestors for over two thousand years. No matter how often her people wandered far away from God, his merciful love brought them back again. Mary herself was the most faithful Daughter of Zion. Her fear of God — or, to put it another way, her extraordinary reverence for the holiness of God — helped her appreciate God's mercy. Spared the taint of original sin by the anticipated merits of Christ's redemption, she was more grateful than anyone, because over time she had a clear vision of what it meant. Because of her Immaculate Conception, her whole life was a prayer. She loved being near God.

That is why she was so shrewd to declare that God's mighty arm disperses the arrogant of mind and heart. Of the seven capital sins, pride is the worst because it makes the self a god.

It's the sin that is furthest away from humility. Proud people do not seek God's mercy, because they do not believe they need it. Small wonder they treat others so mercilessly.

On November 27, 1830, Sr. Catherine Labouré had a second vision of Mary. Our Blessed Mother appeared standing on a globe. Shafts of light extended from her hands toward earth. Surrounding the scene were the words, *O Mary, conceived without sin, pray for us who have recourse to thee.* This was like a picture that was then reversed. On the other side, Sr. Catherine saw the letter *M* with a cross above, it flanked by two hearts, one crowned with thorns and the other pierced with a sword. Twelve stars framed this side of the picture.

Catherine heard a voice telling her to have a medal struck depicting the vision. She persuaded her confessor to bring this message to the archbishop of Paris. Four years later, the archbishop approved the making of 1,500 medals. Countless millions of these medals have been blessed and worn since 1836. Who could ever calculate the number of times the prayer has been said? It is a symbol of humility, not arrogance.

In the mid 1940s, the film *The Song of Bernadette* came out. Jennifer Jones, playing the part of Bernadette, won an Academy Award for her innocent, unaffected portrayal of a peasant teenager who had a vision of Mary in the stone grotto at Lourdes in southern France. The film was a miracle in itself, honestly reporting a profound religious experience and honoring the premise of a vision and the subsequent miracles. In cinematic terms, the film was one of those productions where the actors formed an ensemble, none upstaging the other, yielding a harmonious work of art and faith. The opening lines on the screen produced the right tone for the film: *To those who believe, no explanation is necessary. To those who do not believe, no explanation will suffice.* The humble viewers will be open to faith. Nothing will satisfy the arrogant.

"... he has put down the mighty from their thrones,
and exalted those of low degree;
he has filled the hungry with good things,
and the rich he has sent empty away."

Normally, we do not associate militant images with Mary; she usually excels with the poetry of humility, surrender to God's will, and the beauty of self-giving. Here, however, she identifies with the social conscience of people of faith. We need to remember that barely had Jesus been born that she and Joseph had to flee the Holy Land and become refugees in Egypt. Given the deranged mind of King Herod, that was the only way to keep the infant Jesus from certain death. Since Herod could not tell which male infant was the Christ, he ordered all the newly born male babies be killed.

Matthew's account of the killing of the Holy Innocents reminded him of Jeremiah's report of Rachel mourning. The prophet pictures Jewish slave gangs brutally driven by the Babylonians into exile. As they pass Rachel's tomb, Jeremiah turns to Rachel's grave and comforts her:

"Keep your voice from weeping,
   and your eyes from tears;
for your work will be rewarded, says the LORD,
   and they shall come back from the land of the enemy.
There is hope for your future, says the LORD,
   and your children shall come back to their own country."
                                                    — JER 31:16-17

The Holy Family went into exile carrying the most precious baby ever born. They lived for a time as immigrants in a foreign land, with all the insecurities that came with it. Mary would know the sorrow of Rachel and Jeremiah's frequent sermons against injustice. When they returned to Nazareth, she would hear about the resentments of the Jewish community against Herod and the Roman occupiers, and the wealthy who ignored the poor.

Mary's Song includes the praise of a social conscience. She believed that her little son would defend the humble and hungry. She was convinced that he would bring good news to the poor, freedom for captives, and justice into our world. These words she would hear from her adult son in his first sermon in the synagogue at Nazareth (Lk 4:18-21). Christ's bread miracles — feeding the hungry — reported six times in the Gospels, and his parable about the rich man and poor Lazarus, fulfill the prophetic words of Mary. His institution of the Holy Eucharist became the greatest fulfillment of his total ministry to human hunger.

> *Catholic social teachings maintain there are unchangeable truths, such as the dignity of every human person, and the right to life, from conception to natural death, the primacy of authentic marriage and the family founded upon it, and our obligation in solidarity to one another, and most especially to the poor and needy in our midst. Catholic Social Teaching offers principles which can guide the formation and the exercise of good governance and assist in promoting authentic peace and true economic and social justice.*
> — DEACON KEITH FOURNIER,
> FROM HIS WEB SITE *CATHOLIC ONLINE*

"*He has helped his servant Israel.*
in remembrance of his mercy,
as he spoke to our fathers,
to Abraham and to his posterity forever."

Mary, our mother in faith, concludes her song by citing Abraham, our father in faith. In her culture, unlike our own, memory and tradition were strong attitudes. Not only do God's people have vivid memories of God's mighty deeds on their behalf, they believe that God is the primary "rememberer" of his mercies and promises:

"Can a mother forget her suckling child, that she should be without compassion on the son of her womb? Even these may forget, yet I will not forget you. Behold, I have graven you upon the palms of my hands."

— Is 49:15-16

At the Last Supper, after Jesus instituted the Eucharist, he said, "Do this in remembrance of me" (Luke 22:19). From that very moment, the Eucharist became the living memory of the risen Christ among us. Where there is Eucharist, there is the Church, as the People of God. Where there is Eucharist, there is the ordained priesthood. On Holy Thursday night, Mary's Son

---

THE ROSARY MEANS "CROWN OF ROSES"

All the idle moments of one's life can be sanctified, thanks to the rosary. As we walk the streets we pray with the Rosary hidden in our hand or in our pocket. Driving an automobile, the little knobs under the steering wheel can serve as counters to the decades. While waiting to be served at a luncheon, or waiting for a train, or in a store, or while playing dummy at bridge, or when conversation or a lecture lags — all these moments can be sanctified and made to serve inner peace, thanks to a prayer that enables one to pray at all times and under all circumstances. If you wish to convert anyone to the fullness of the knowledge of Our Lord and of his Mystical Body, then teach him the Rosary. One of two things will happen. Either he will stop saying the Rosary — or he will get the gift of faith.

— Archbishop Fulton J. Sheen, *The World's First Love*
(Ignatius Press, 1996), p. 184

---

created the sacraments of Eucharist and priesthood and brought into being the Church he had promised, the Church that would be publicly manifested by the Holy Spirit at Pentecost.

All the divine promises and memories stored up by God's people of the first covenant now are wondrously come to life in the sacraments Christ gave us in the Upper Room. We never fail to do Eucharist in memory of Jesus, not as a recollection of something past but a memory that makes Christ's Body and Blood present today. Each time this happens, the Church grows in holiness and closer to the final new creation at the end of history.

Each time we go to Communion, let us walk with Mary; she also received her Son in a new, sacramental way as she participated in the Breaking of the Bread in her last years on earth. Take her by the hand and feel her reverence for her Son. Watch her take him again into her life. Hear her say "Amen" with a silence and memory that only a mother can retain. Then let her bring you to him.

We conclude our reflection on Mary's Song with a meditation from St. Bede the Venerable.

> *Therefore it is an excellent and fruitful custom of holy Church that we should sing Mary's hymn at the time of evening prayer. By meditating on the incarnation, our devotion is kindled, and by remembering the example of God's Mother, we are encouraged to lead a life of virtue. Such virtues are best achieved in the evening. We are weary after a day's work and worn out by our distractions. The time for rest is near, and our minds are ready for contemplation.*
>
> *— LH* VOL. III, P. 1439

CLOSING PRAYER

Eternal Father,
You inspired the Virgin Mary, mother of your Son,

to visit Elizabeth and assist her in her need.
Keep us open to the working of your Spirit,
and with Mary may we praise you forever.

FOR REFLECTION

1. What are your favorite Christmas carols, and what do they tell you about Jesus and how to live the Christian life?
2. Which lines of Mary's Song appeal most to you, and how do they enrich your prayer life?
3. What are some ways you have found to give of yourself to God?

FOR CONTEMPLATION

Mary carried a little child, she caressed him, she embraced him, she whispered most beautiful words to him and adored him saying: My Master, give yourself to me for me to embrace you.

As you are my son, I will rock you with my lullabies. I am your mother but I will give honor to you. My son, I have engendered you, but you are older than I am. My Lord, I have carried you in my womb, but you sustain me on my feet.

May my Magnificat be for you who is older than everyone, and nevertheless, having been made a child, you descended to me. Sit on my knees, in spite of the whole world, the highest peaks and the deepest abyss hanging from you.

— FROM "ST. EPHREM THE SYRIAN, HYMN 18";
CLAIRE RUSSELL, *GLIMPSES OF THE CHURCH FATHERS*
(SCEPTER PRESS), PP. 107-108

GOING FORWARD IN YOUR PRAYER

If I don't go into the desert to meet God, then I have nothing to say when I go into the market-place. I could only survive my work as Archbishop... if I have allocated so much of the day to prayer. That has to be done, in my case, early in the morning. I don't think I could survive in my job unless I had that half hour. It has become very important to me.
— CARDINAL BASIL HUME, FROM
WHISPERS IN THE LOGGIA (ONLINE), JUNE 16, 2009

In this book on prayer, we began with Jesus and concluded with Mary, two icons of prayer. We pictured Jesus being taught to pray by his mother, Mary; saw him brought to the synagogue services by Joseph, where he learned to sing the Psalms and heard the rabbi preach about God's goodness to Israel and the hope for the Messiah. We recalled their family pilgrimages to the Temple in Jerusalem, his "Father's house." Christ's house in Nazareth was a home of prayer.

Then we followed Christ's path of prayer in the desert, on the mountain, and before major decisions and healings. You may recall that his prayer life so fascinated the apostles that they asked him to teach them to pray. They had already been instructed in prayer by their parents and the customs of their faith, yet the awe that radiated from Jesus at prayer moved them to desire such prayer for themselves. Jesus responded with the best prayer ever composed, the *Our Father*. Here is a prayer with seven petitions that will never be exhausted in the souls of those who meditate on them. It is a short prayer with oceans of depth and a deceptive simplicity that only people with faith can appreciate.

As you continued this journey, we opened God's prayer book, the Psalms. It is no mistake that in a theology library, the most commentaries are about the Gospels and the Psalms. For centuries, people have hungered to know how to pray the Psalms. Typically, monasteries, convents, and seminaries arrange their days around singing the Psalms in the Liturgy of the Hours. Every Eucharist contains a psalm as a response to the first reading. We found some answers to questions about the perennial love of these prayer songs from ancient Israel, but even in our secular culture, the Psalms seem more appropriate than ever. While these 150 prayers contain some cultural mysteries and historical puzzles, they touch virtually every human feeling possible. Jesus knew this. So has the Church, from Christ's time to our own era.

Next, we partnered with some saints (the author's favorites, of course!) — not necessarily for everyone's tastes, needs, and hopes. But in this mosaic of durable holy men and women, we can still find a common humanity struggling with faith and filled with a passion for God.

Many of us have been intrigued that Augustine's greatest forty years were passed in a backwater in north Africa. There he was in Hippo, not far from the formidable Sahara, and very far from Rome. Think of his lucky parishioners: mostly working class, far from the madding crowd, yet gathering on Sundays to hear hundreds — yes, thousands — of some of the greatest homilies ever delivered.

Think of him in his study, writing classics such as his *Confessions*, *The City of God*, and commentaries on the Psalms and John's Gospel. All of his homilies and other writings flow from a heart and mind saturated with prayer, balanced with his ability to give down-home advice to the Lady Proba about just that subject. He simply could not avoid the sublime — nor should we.

After that, we met Anselm, who framed one of the best axioms about prayer ever written. Very simple, very memorable, and very demanding: "Believe, that you may understand." That should be inscribed somewhere in every Catholic home, parish church, school, religious education center, and seminary. It is faith that makes prayer work. Certainly, the presence and action of the Holy Spirit inspires us with this needed faith, so we can believe for the sake of understanding what it means.

Many people like to use a "conversation with God" model when they pray. If that is you, St. Catherine of Siena will assure you this is quite effective. You don't need to aspire to her mystical revelations, but you clearly can dialogue with Christ any time you pray. Prayer is a relationship with God. So why not converse with the One you love?

Church history is replete with sometimes surprising cases of soldiers who become saints. Veterans of our wars often return with a deeper faith than they had at enlistment. Ignatius arrived at prayer while his war-torn leg took a year to mend. It just so happened that he had an orderly mind that created spiritual exercises, directing me and you through a process of prayer that has molded people in sanctity for over four centuries. It's still remarkable — and readily available.

Teresa of Ávila should prove helpful to you if you have a feisty personality. (Despite protests to the contrary, that trait has prompted prayer growth more that some people would think possible!) Teresa was no pushover. She bargained over properties with a zeal that would embarrass most of us. But, oh, how she could pray and approach God with fire . . . which Our Lord transformed into memorable holiness.

In thinking of our intensely personalized culture, no doubt Francis de Sales' approach to prayer is aptly suitable for us today. He would be puzzled by the idea that "one size fits all." His flexible but authentic advice on prayer, adapted to a variety of gifts and roles, fits our times remarkably well.

I first came across Thérèse of Lisieux in my novitiate days; as a young seminarian, I fell for her "Little Way" of love in every act and her promises to help us. Her resolve to become "Love in the heart of the Church" always stirs me to prayer. From all appearances, I'm not alone!

Finally, we "tasted again for the first time" Mary's Song, the *Magnificat*. Before her sharing in the paschal mystery, Mary contemplated the Word made flesh — from *her* flesh. Her prayer canticle is composed while Jesus is in her womb.

Most of the few quotes from her are prayers, such as her farewell line, "Do whatever Jesus tells you" (cf. Jn 2:5). (It's fascinating for our imaginations to picture Mary with John in their home, overlooking the city of Ephesus.) But, while many of our prayers are vocal, Mary is best recalled for her silence — a contemplative woman. So it's fitting that we finish this book with her model of contemplative prayer as an example for all of us to follow, in whatever manner the Holy Spirit may move you.

No one of us can achieve all of these ideals and dreams. But we can all benefit in some way with each witness of prayer. Remember that all of the saints' prayer styles and content have one goal: loving union with our Father in heaven, through Jesus Christ, in the Holy Spirit. To that end, we close this book with another line from Cardinal Hume: "The best way to pray is the way that suits you."

Notes

Notes

Notes

More Inspiration and Insight from Father McBride

Father McBride's eloquent style is sure to inspire a desire to know the teachings of the Faith more completely and to live them more fully. Enjoy these other titles from Father McBride.

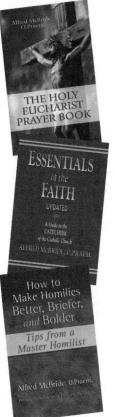

The Holy Eucharist Prayer Book,
by Alfred McBride, O.Praem.

978-1-59276-147-0 (ID#T198), Hardback, 64 pp., $6.95

Beautiful prayer book of original and traditional prayers to help prepare for the celebration of Mass and Eucharistic adoration.

Essentials of the Faith, Updated: A Guide to the Catechism,
by Alfred McBride, O.Praem.

978-1-93170-953-8 (ID#T30), Paperback, 224 pp., $12.95

This essential guide delivers its timeless teachings with relevance and applicability to real life. Accessible, topical, and easy to use.

How to Make Homilies Better, Briefer, and Bolder, *by Alfred McBride, O.Praem.*

978-1-59276-198-2 (ID#T249), Paperback, 160 pp., $15.95

Blending practical, proven strategies, this guide encapsulates 50 years of homily mastery from the author.

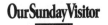